READING ABOUT SCIENCE
Skills and Concepts

John F. Mongillo
Ray Broekel
Beth S. Atwood
Donald L. Buchholz
Albert B. Carr
Claudia Cornett
Jacqueline L. Harris
Vivian Zwaik

Special Reading Consultant
Roger Farr
    Professor of Education
    Indiana University

Phoenix Learning Resources
New York

G

PHOTO CREDITS

ISBN 0—7915—1207—X

(Previously ISBN 0—07—002427—8)

AUTHORS

John F. Mongillo
Editor in Chief, Science Department
Webster Division
McGraw-Hill Book Company
New York, New York

Dr. Ray Broekel
Author and Consultant
Ipswich, Massachusetts

Beth S. Atwood
Writer and Reading Consultant
Durham, Connecticut

Donald L. Buchholz
Developer of Curriculum Materials
Honolulu, Hawaii

Albert B. Carr
Professor of Science Education
University of Hawaii
Honolulu, Hawaii

Claudia Cornett
Assistant Professor of Education
Wittenberg University
Springfield, Ohio

Jacqueline L. Harris
Writer and Science Editor
Wethersfield, Connecticut

Vivian Zwaik
Writer and Educational Consultant
Glen Head, New York

Contributing Writers

Rita Harkins Dickinson
Special Education Instructor
Rio Salado Community College
Phoenix, Arizona

Myra J. Goldberg
Reading Consultant
Rye, New York

Adrienne Ballard Taylor
Junior High School Science Teacher
Black Mountain School
Cave Creek, Arizona

Bruce Tone
Editorial Associate
School of Education
Indiana University
Bloomington, Indiana

Dr. Clifford Watson
Staff Coordinator
Region 1
Detroit Public Schools
Detroit, Michigan

Reviewers

PRONUNCIATION GUIDE

Some words in this book may be unfamiliar to you and difficult for you to pronounce. These words are printed in italics. Then, they are spelled according to the way they are said, or pronounced. This phonetic spelling appears in parentheses next to the words. The pronunciation guide below will help you say the words.

ă	pat	î	dear, deer, fierce, mere	p	pop	zh	garage, pleasure; vision
ā	aid, fey, pay			r	roar		
â	air, care, wear	j	judge	s	miss, sauce, see	ə	about, silent pencil, lemon, circus
ä	father	k	cat, kick, pique	sh	dish, ship		
b	bib	l	lid, needle	t	tight		
ch	church	m	am, man, mum	th	path, thin	ər	butter
d	deed	n	no, sudden	*th*	bathe, this		
ĕ	pet, pleasure	ng	thing	ŭ	cut, rough		
ē	be, bee, easy, leisure	ŏ	horrible, pot	û	circle, firm, heard, term, turn, urge, word		
		ō	go, hoarse, row, toe				STRESS
f	fast, fife, off, phase, rough	ô	alter, caught, for, paw	v	cave, valve, vine		Primary stress ′
g	gag			w	with		**bi·ol′o·gy**
h	hat	oi	boy, noise, oil	y	yes		[bī ŏl′ejē]
hw	which	ou	cow, out	yōō	abuse, use		Secondary stress′
ĭ	pit	ŏŏ	took	z	rose, size, xylophone, zebra		**bi′o·log′i·cal**
ī	by, guy, pie	ōō	boot, fruit				[bī′elŏj′ĭkel]

TABLE OF CONTENTS

The world of science is a world of observing, exploring, predicting, reading, experimenting, testing, and recording. It is a world of trying and failing and trying again until, at last, you succeed. In the world of science, there is always some exciting discovery to be made and something new to explore.

In this book, you will learn about some of these explorations and discoveries. Through these readings about science, you will have a chance to join the crew of the *Alvin* and explore the strange world beneath the sea. You may hop aboard a hot-air balloon and float across the Atlantic Ocean or track cougars through the Rocky Mountains. You will learn that science is an important part of your life—and that reading about science is fun.

Three Areas of Science

READING ABOUT SCIENCE explores three areas of science: life science, earth-space science, and physical science. Each book in this series contains a unit on each of the three areas. Although there are different areas of science, it is important to remember that each area is related to the others in some way and that all areas are important to people.

Life science is the study of living things. Life scientists explore the world of plants, animals, and humans. Their goal is to find out how living things depend upon each other for survival and to observe how they live and interact in their environments, or surroundings.

The general area of life science includes many specialized areas, such as botany, zoology, and ecology. *Botanists* work mainly with plants. *Zoologists* work mostly with animals. *Ecologists* are scientists who study the effects of air pollution, water pollution, and noise pollution on living things.

Earth-space science is the study of our Earth and other bodies in the solar system. Some earth-space scientists are *meteorologists,* who study climate and weather; *geologists,* who study the earth, the way it was formed and its makeup, rocks and fossils, earthquakes, and volcanoes; *oceanographers,* who study currents, waves, and life in the oceans of the world; and *astronomers,* who study the solar system, including the sun and other stars, moons, and planets.

Physical science is the study of matter and energy. *Physicists* are physical scientists who explore topics such as matter, atoms, and nuclear energy. Other physical scientists study sound, magnetism, heat, light, electricity, water, and air. *Chemists* develop the substances used in medicine, clothing, food, and many other things.

All of these areas of science influence our everyday life. For example, our transportation and communications systems depend on the work of physical scientists. Together, physical scientists, earth-space scientists, and life scientists search for ways to solve problems and improve the quality of our everyday life.

In your reading, you may discover that there is one area of science that you like especially. The bibliography in the back of this book is divided into life, earth-space, and physical sciences. The books that are suggested will take you on more adventures in the world of science.

Reading Science Materials

Some students are nervous about taking courses in science. They think that science is too difficult, and so they give up even before they begin.

Think about this. Do you enjoy the world around you? Do you ever wonder why clouds have so many different shapes and what keeps planes up in the air? Did you ever want to explore a cave or find out why volcanoes erupt or why the earth shakes? If you can answer yes to any of those questions and if you are willing to read and think and investigate carefully the world around you, then you can do well in science and enjoy it, too!

Reading science materials is different from reading a magazine or a novel. You must take your time and think about what you are reading. Remember that science materials contain special vocabulary words. You will know some words. Other words may be familiar to you, but you may be unsure of their meanings. And still other words may be totally unfamiliar. It is these unfamiliar words in particular that make science reading seem difficult.

Steps to Follow

The suggestions that follow will help you use this book:

A.   Study the photo or drawing that goes with the story. Read the title and the sentences that are printed in blue. These are all clues to what the story is about.

B. Study the words for the story in the list of Words to Know in the back of this book. You will find it easier to read the story if you understand the meanings of these words. Many times, you will find the meaning of the word right in the story.

When reading the story, look for clues to important words or ideas. Vocabulary words appear in a special print. Sometimes words or phrases are underlined. Pay special attention to these clues.

C. Read the story carefully. Think about what you are reading. Are any of the ideas in the story things that you have heard or read about before?

D. As you read, ask yourself questions. For example, "Why did the electricity go off?" "What caused the bears to turn green?" Many times, your questions are answered later in the story. Questioning helps you to understand what the author is saying. Asking questions also gets you ready for what comes next in the story.

E. Pay special attention to diagrams, charts, and other visual aids. They will often help you to understand the story better.

F. After you read the story slowly and carefully, you are ready to answer the questions on the Questions page. If the book you have is part of a classroom set, you should write your answers in a special notebook or on paper that you can keep in a folder. Do not write in this book without your teacher's permission.

Put your name, the title of the story, and its page number on a sheet of paper. Read each question carefully. Record the question number and your answer on your answer paper.

The questions in this book check for the following kinds of comprehension, or understanding:

1. *Science vocabulary comprehension.* This kind of question asks you to remember the meaning of a word or term used in the story.

2. *Literal comprehension.* This kind of question asks you to remember certain facts that are given in the story. For example, the story might state that a snake was over 5 meters long. A literal question would ask you: "How long was the snake?"

3. *Interpretive comprehension.* This kind of question asks you to think about the story. To answer the question, you must decide what the author means, not what is said, or stated, in the story. For example, you may be

asked what the *main idea* of the story is or what happened first, or what *caused* something to happen in the story.

4. *Applied comprehension.* This kind of question asks you to use what you have read to (1) solve a new problem, (2) interpret a chart or graph; or (3) put a certain topic under its correct heading, or category.

You should read each question carefully. You may go back to the story to help you find the answer. The questions are meant to help you learn how to read science better.

G.   When you complete the Questions page, turn it in to your teacher. Or, with your teacher's permission, check your answers against the answer key in the *Teacher's Guide.* If you made a mistake, find out what you did wrong. Practice answering that kind of question, and you will do better the next time.

H.   Turn to the directions that tell you how to keep your Progress Charts. If you are not supposed to write in this book, you may make a copy of each chart to keep in your READING ABOUT SCIENCE folder or notebook. You may be surprised to see how well you can read science.

Special Sections

There are some special sections that follow each of the three science units.

People to Know is about a person or a group of people who have done something special in the field of life science, earth-space science, or physical science. Some examples are Margaret Seddon, astronaut; Jacques Cousteau, undersea explorer; Benjamin Banneker, astronomer; and Mary Jean Currier, wildlife scientist.

Places to Go takes you on visits to aquariums, zoos, space centers, and museums all over the United States and in Canada.

Puzzles to Do includes crossword puzzles, hidden-word games, and mazes on many different topics in science.

Science Adventures gives you a chance to investigate interesting topics such as solar energy, making fossils, and extrasensory perception.

The last unit in the book is a special unit called Careers in Science. This unit gives you an opportunity to investigate hundreds of science-related careers.

You may decide to make science your lifelong hobby or even your career. Whatever you do, the authors of READING ABOUT SCIENCE hope that this book will help you discover the joys of science.

LIFE SCIENCE

Deer have no permanent home. They spend their lives moving about within an area called their "home range." During the winter, they cluster in sheltered valleys, living on bark and other scarce vegetation. If there is not enough food to support the deer population, many of them starve. This is one reason a carefully controlled hunting season is permitted in many wilderness regions.

What Color Are Polar Bears?

What color are polar bears? White, of course! Why, then, were polar bears in a certain zoo turning green?

The keeper in the San Diego Zoo blinked her eyes. She couldn't believe what she was seeing. The polar bears had a *greenish* look! They were no longer white, as everyone knows polar bears should be. After this discovery, greenish-looking polar bears were also reported in several other zoos.

That is when scientists were called. The scientists discovered that the green color was caused by plants called *algae* (ăl′ jē). Algae are simple plants found in fresh or salt water and in damp places on land. They use sunlight to make their own food and are an important food source for animals that live in the water.

When the scientists used microscopes to inspect the bears' fur, they found that the algae were actually growing inside the hollow shafts of the stiff hair on the bears' bodies. Even inside the hairs, the plants received sufficient sunlight to live and grow and give the bears' fur a greenish look.

The scientists examined the algae and discovered that they belonged to a common freshwater species that grows in lakes or swimming pools. The scientists had a theory that the algae in the bears' pools probably got into the hair shafts through breaks in the hair tips.

Although the algae did not harm the bears, the scientists thought it best to use a salt solution to kill the plants. Visitors to a zoo would expect to see white polar bears—certainly not green ones.

1. The word *algae* is used to describe simple _____ found in fresh or salt water and in damp places on land.

2. What did scientists use to inspect the hairs on the bears' bodies?

3. The polar bears that turned green were living in _____.

4. According to the story, in order to survive, algae *must* have
   a. sunlight.
   b. fresh water.
   c. salt.

5. The natural home of polar bears is the freezing cold Arctic. Their true color is useful because it
   a. camouflages, or hides, them from enemies.
   b. makes it easier for scientists to spot them.
   c. attracts algae, which help the bears' fur to grow.

6. The story says that the scientists had a theory about how the algae got into the bears' fur. The word *theory* means about the same as
   a. proof.   b. idea.   c. solution.

7. The algae found in the bears' fur belonged to _____ species.
   a. an unusual
   b. a harmful
   c. a common

8. For some reason, your green houseplants are wilting and dying. It could be that
   a. there is not enough salt in the plants' soil.
   b. the plants are not being watered properly.
   c. they are not located in a place that is dark enough for green plants.

Save the Wolf!

How do wolves keep other animals from starving?

Many years ago, large, dog-like mammals called wolves lived and hunted in many parts of Mexico, Canada, and the United States. But, by the early 1970s, wolves had disappeared from many places. The red wolf, for example, was greatly reduced in numbers. Many of these wolves were hunted and killed. Also, no steps were taken to keep the wolves from breeding with their western relatives, the coyotes. Today, wolves are an endangered species, that is, they are in danger of becoming *extinct* (ĭk stĭngkt′), or dying out completely.

Scientists feel that wolves should be protected, because they are an important link in a *food chain*. Every living plant or animal is part of a food chain. A food chain begins with the sun. Green plants use sunlight to make their own food. Then, the green plants are eaten by small animals, such as rabbits, which are then eaten by larger animals.

Grass, deer, and wolves are an example of one food chain. Wolves are an important part of the chain because they are *predators* (prĕd′ə tərz). Predators get their food by hunting other animals. Wolves hunt animals such as deer, elk, and caribou. By doing this, they help preserve the balance of nature.

If the wolf is not saved from extinction, elk and deer herds may increase to such an extent that, in time, these animals may eat up all the available plant food in an area. As a result, many animals would starve to death.

Wolves keep the population of a herd in balance. They control the size of the herd by hunting and feeding on the old, crippled, and sick animals. So predators such as wolves play an essential part in a food chain and help to preserve our wildlife.

1. An animal that is in danger of dying out completely could soon become _____.

2. Animals that get their food by hunting other animals are called _____.

3. Scientists are concerned with protecting the wolf because it helps _____ the balance of nature.

4. In the food chain described in the story, wolves play an important role in the _____ of the chain.
    a. first stage   b. second stage   c. third stage

5. Which of the following has *not* led to a decrease in the number of red wolves?
    a. letting them breed with coyotes
    b. poisoning them with plant spray   c. hunting and killing them

6. Which of the following animals would *most* likely be a predator?
    a. a deer   b. a fox   c. a rabbit

Use the table to answer questions 7 and 8.

THREATENED & ENDANGERED SPECIES ACT OF 1973
Updated as of 1987 by U.S. Fish & Wildlife

Species or Kind	United States	Foreign Countries	Total
Mammals	38	276	313
Birds	60	163	223
Reptiles	19	79	98
Amphibians	7	9	16
Fish	72	11	83
Snails	8	1	9
Clams	28	2	30
Crustaceans	6	0	6
Insects	13	0	13
Totals	251	540	791

7. On this list, the species in *least* danger of becoming extinct are _____.

8. There are more kinds of endangered _____ in the United States than in foreign countries.
    a. birds   b. snails   c. fish

Dragons Alive!

Of all the known species of reptiles, the monitor lizard is the largest and heaviest species.

Reptiles (rĕp'tīlz') are cold-blooded animals with lungs and backbones. They are covered with scales, or horny plates, and usually lay eggs. One *species* (spē'shēz'), or type, of reptile, the monitor lizard, ranges in length from about 2 to 4 meters and can weigh as much as 115 kilograms. Its forked tongue is long and slender, and it can turn its head in all directions.

The Komodo dragon is the largest of all known monitor lizards. Discovered in 1912 on the small island of Komodo in Indonesia, this lizard is extremely active and savage. It has saw-like teeth that can tear its prey—wild pigs, small deer, goats, and monkeys—into tiny, bite-sized pieces. The Komodo uses its powerful claws to dig holes for shelter. Its mighty tail is as long as its head and body put together. The lizard uses its tail as a weapon to fight off its enemies.

When the female Komodo lays her eggs in August, each one is about the size of a softball. Once they hatch, baby Komodos grow rapidly, and, by the age of 5 years they are fully grown. However, Komodos continue to gain weight because of their tremendous appetites.

The Komodo dragon is at home on land and in the water. During the day, it hunts in the rain forests and lowlands. On hot days, the lizard can cool itself in the water while it lazily digests a meal. At night, the Komodo sleeps in holes it has dug or among rocks or tree roots.

The Komodo dragon is considered to be a relative of the extinct giant lizards that roamed Earth before the existence of humans. Therefore, the government of Indonesia has passed laws protecting this living dragon.

1. The story describes _____ as cold-blooded animals with lungs and backbones. They are covered with scales, or horny plates.

2. The Komodo dragon is the largest of all known _____ lizards.

3. Which of the following describes the Komodo dragon?
   a. active and savage   b. harmless and lazy
   c. huge and timid

4. The Komodo dragon seems to prefer eating
   a. plants.   b. meat.   c. fish.

5. If you saw a Komodo dragon that was about 4 meters long, you could be fairly certain that the lizard
   a. would continue to grow in length.   b. was about 3 years old.
   c. was an adult

Use the chart to answer questions 6, 7, and 8.

THE KOMODO DRAGON

Physical Feature	Description	Use
Skin	Rough, scaly	To protect itself
Teeth	Sawlike	To tear prey into small pieces
Claws	Powerful	To dig holes for shelter
Tail	As long as head and body together	To defend itself against enemies

6. Which physical feature of the Komodo dragon could be compared to a steak knife used by humans?

7. Humans use shovels and bulldozers to build houses and apartment buildings for shelter. The Komodo dragon uses its _____.

8. Humans use their hands, but the Komodo dragon uses its tail to _____.

Spiders Have Incredible Instincts

What do horses, cats, and spiders have in common? They are animals.

Spiders are misunderstood animals. First, they are not insects, as most people think. All insects have six legs, but spiders have eight. Spiders have only two body parts—the head and the abdomen—while insects have a third part called the thorax.

Second, most spiders are not poisonous. There are only two kinds, or *species* (spē'shēz'), of poisonous spiders in the United States. These two species are the black widow and the brown recluse. Even most tarantulas are not poisonous.

Of the 30,000 different species of spiders ranging in size from 32 centimeters to 61 centimeters, only about one-half spin webs. All spiders produce silk, but each species has its own special way to use the silk. The web spinners use the silk to weave webs where they capture their prey. Probably the most familiar web is the circular web of the garden spider.

Other spiders make silky nets to drop over their victims. Another species sends out a single sticky strand of silk like a fishing line. When a fly is caught in the silk, the spider hauls in its "fish." Then the spider usually bites the insect and injects poison into it to paralyze or kill it. The spider then sucks out the victim's body juices. Because the spider has no mouth parts for chewing, it cannot eat solid food.

Many spiders have very poor eyesight, but one species, the jumping spider, has eight eyes. Jumping spiders can see perfectly in every direction. These spiders are also called "tiger spiders," because they sneak up and leap on their victims the way a tiger does.

1. Each different kind of spider belongs to a different _____.

2. How many legs do spiders have?
   a. three
   b. six
   c. eight

3. The brown recluse and the _____ are the two poisonous spiders found in the United States.

4. According to the story, web spinners use their silky webs to
   a. sleep in.
   b. catch food.
   c. hide themselves.

5. The story leads you to believe that some spiders eat juices from
   a. fish.
   b. people.
   c. flies.

6. If you found a spider among some plants, its web would appear
   a. round.
   b. long.
   c. thick.

7. How would you rate the jumping spider's ability to see?

1 2 3	4 5 6 7	8 9 10
POOR	GOOD	VERY GOOD

   a. 2
   b. 6
   c. 10

8. Under which of the following headings would you list spiders?
   a. Clever Predators
   b. Headless Animals
   c. Helpful Insects

Helping Baby Fish Survive

Now baby fish have a better chance for survival.

Most kinds of fish lay hundreds or thousands of eggs. But most of the newly hatched fish are eaten by predators and do not have a chance to become fully grown. Now, Jeffrey Marliave, a marine biologist at the Vancouver Public Aquarium in British Columbia, Canada, has invented a device that protects baby fish.

Marliave's invention is a kind of *incubator* (ĭn'kyə bā'tər) for newly hatched fish. An incubator is a device that is used to promote the growth and development of young living organisms. It does this by providing the organism with a protective environment.

The incubator looks something like a big tub with a cone-shaped screen on one side and a rudder on the opposite side. The incubator is filled with newly hatched fish and then dropped into a body of water. The rudder directs the screened side of the incubator so that it faces the tide currents in the ocean water. In this way, the seawater can enter through the screen and circulate through the incubator. Tiny bits of plants and animals contained in the water serve as food for the young fish. The incubator also protects the baby fish from predators until they grow to full size and can take care of themselves. Then the fish can be released directly into the water or can be raised to a larger size and sold as food.

Marliave's invention could be used to help restock fishing grounds with certain saltwater fish that are popular with fishers. One such food fish is the lingcod found in Puget Sound.

1. Marliave's invention that protects baby fish is a kind of
   _____ .

2. According to the story, most baby fish are eaten by _____ .

3. Opposite the screen side of the incubator is a _____ .

4. How do the baby fish get fed in the incubator?
   a. Food is dropped into the incubator.
   b. They eat tiny pieces of plants and animals in the seawater.
   c. The incubator opens so that they can catch their own food.

5. The incubator serves to protect the baby fish from predators because
   a. its cone shape scares predators away.
   b. predators cannot fit through the screen.
   c. fishers trap the predators in the incubator.

6. The screen acts most like
   a. a filter.
   b. a door.
   c. bait.

7. Under which of the following headings would you list Marliave's invention?
   a. A Watertight Machine for Raising Baby Fish
   b. A Jail for Predators of Baby Fish
   c. A Life-Saving Device for Baby Fish

8. How would you rate the chances for survival of most newly hatched fish in open water?

1	2	3		4	5	6	7		8	9	10
	POOR				GOOD					EXCELLENT	

   a. 2   b. 6   c. 10

Open Your Mouth, John Dory

Who is John Dory? A fish, of course.

In terms of appearance, the John Dory is a unique fish. In the center of its body is a large, round black spot that is surrounded by a yellow ring. According to one legend, this spot is a thumbprint left over from Saint Peter when he took a coin out of the fish's mouth. When full grown, the John Dory may reach a length of about 60 centimeters. There are many stories about how this fish got its name. According to one story, fishers along the Adriatic Sea in Europe named their catch *il janitore*. In English, this name sounds something like "Johnny Dory," which, when shortened, becomes "John Dory."

The John Dory lives in the shallow oceans off the coasts of southern Europe and Africa. It swims at depths where it can be caught by fishers. And since it is an edible and good-tasting fish, fishers like to bring up lots of John Dories in their nets.

The John Dory is a *predator* (prĕd′ə tər), that is, it lives by capturing and feeding on other animals. This predator has an unusual way of catching its prey. The John Dory has jaws that can separate from each other. When the predator gets close enough to its prey, it drops its lower jaw. Its mouth is now shaped somewhat like a large tube. The John Dory then sucks the fish it is pursuing into its tube-shaped mouth and snaps its lower jaw back to its upper jaw. This done, *il janitore* swims off eating its prey as if nothing has happened.

1. An animal that captures and lives off other animals is called a
    _____.

2. About how long can a full-grown John Dory be?

3. Why do fishers like to catch John Dories?
    a. They can be used as bait.
    b. They are predators.
    c. They are good to eat.

4. How do you know when the John Dory is ready to capture its
    prey?
    a. It snarls and bites.
    b. It drops its lower jaw.
    c. It dives down into the sea.

5. As the John Dory eats its prey, its upper jaw is
    a. opened wide.
    b. held in place.
    c. dropped down.

6. What makes the John Dory unusual looking?
    a. its yellow eyes
    b. its large jaws
    c. its black spot

7. Which of the following might you compare to the way in which
    a John Dory uses its mouth?
    a. a person drinking with a straw
    b. a bird tearing up an insect
    c. a person using a fork and a spoon

8. Under which of the following headings would you list the John
    Dory?
    a. Deep-Water Fish
    b. Predatory Fish
    c. Inedible Fish

Cattails: The Everything Plant

Beauty, food, and energy—cattails have it all.

Most people tend to think of cattails as merely pretty. Clumps of these graceful, bushy spikes add to the natural beauty of marshes and swamps. They can be just the right touch in a flower arrangement.

But soon, cattails may be known as "the everything plant." This is what some people in Minnesota think. Minnesota has a lot of swamps and a lot of cattails growing wild. Scientists at the University of Minnesota have been testing cattails. They have found that the plants could be a rich source of energy and food. Cattails could also provide the raw material from which to make paper.

The bushy top of the cattail is one energy source. Scientists have found that the bushy tops can be pressed into small pellets or bricks, which can then be burned as fuel. In addition, chemical processes can change the tops into alcohol or methane—both fuels.

The best food source is in the cattails' *rhizomes* (rī'zōmz'). Rhizomes are root-like stems that grow under or along the ground. Chemical testing of cattail rhizomes shows that they are rich in sugar and starch. The rhizomes can be used to make flour or

animal food. The starch and sugar in the rhizomes can be made into alcohol. The leaves and stems of the cattail plant can be ground up and used to make paper.

So do the people of Minnesota plan to cover their state with cattails? Not really. But many scientists do think that large fields of cattails could supply energy for small towns. In fact, some scientists think that cattails could supply 7 percent of Minnesota's energy by the year 2000.

1. Root-like stems that grow under or along the ground are called
   _____.

2. The cattail plant can be found in
   a. bricks.   b. swamps.   c. alcohol.

3. Which of the following is *true,* according to the story?
   a. The state of Minnesota is covered with fields of cattails.
   b. Cattails may someday supply energy for small towns.
   c. By the year 2000, cattails will supply most of Minnesota's energy.

4. In order to use the cattail plant to make paper, it is necessary to
   a. change the tops of the plant into alcohol.
   b. grind up the leaves and stems.
   c. treat the rhizomes with a special chemical.

5. In the story, cattails are called "the everything plant." They probably got this name
   a. as a result of scientific experiments on the plants.
   b. because people were eating the plants.
   c. after they were found growing all over Minnesota.

6. Before the bushy tops of the cattail can be used as an energy source, they must first be
   a. burned.
   b. pressed into small pellets.
   c. ground up into a flour-like substance.

7. Based on this story, which of the following words does *not* describe cattails?
   a. pretty   b. useful   c. rare

8. Under which heading would you classify both methane and alcohol?
   a. Fuels   b. Plants   c. Starches

Green Sea Turtles Make a Comeback

Green sea turtles are reappearing in ocean waters throughout the world.

Sandy beaches are the *breeding grounds* of the green sea turtle. Breeding grounds are places where animals and fish go to mate and lay their eggs. The green sea turtle digs a nest in the sandy beach away from the water's edge. After laying about 100 eggs, the turtle covers the nest with sand. About 2 months later, the eggs hatch and the baby turtles, each about 7 centimeters long, immediately head for the sea. On their way, the newly hatched turtles are preyed upon by hungry birds, crabs, or raccoons. Even those sea turtles that reach water are not always safe. Some of them are eaten by hungry fish along the shore.

Green turtles are found in tropical or warm regions throughout the world. One place where green turtles lay their eggs is on islands in the Sulu Sea off the coast of Malaysia. For years, island people had collected turtle eggs because their shells fetched a good price and they could be used in cooking. In fact, so many eggs were collected that fewer and fewer turtles hatched each year, and the green sea turtle was in danger of becoming *extinct* (ĭk stĭngkt′), or disappearing completely from the earth.

So the government of Malaysia decided to buy the islands and name them Turtle Islands National Park. The eggs were now protected by wildlife services and game wardens. Records were kept of the number of eggs laid and the turtles that hatched. During a 6-year period, more than 1 million green sea turtles made it to the water!

1. Places where animals and fish go to mate and lay their eggs are called _____.

2. Baby sea turtles are about _____ centimeters long.

3. Newly hatched green sea turtles are in danger of being
   a. buried in sand.
   b. preyed upon.
   c. drowned.

4. The green sea turtle seems to prefer a _____ climate.

5. What led to the reduction in the number of green sea turtles hatched on the islands in the Sulu Sea?
   a. People collected the turtle eggs to sell.
   b. Turtle eggs were washed away by ocean currents.
   c. Fish came ashore and ate the turtle eggs.

6. The Malaysian government bought the islands in the Sulu Sea because it wanted to save the wildlife from extinction.
   a. True
   b. False
   c. The story does not say.

7. Of the following places, you are most likely to find green sea turtles off the coast of
   a. Maine.   b. Oregon.   c. Florida.

8. How would you rate the chances of the Turtle Islands' baby sea turtles for reaching the sea?

1 2 3	4 5 6 7	8 9 10
FAIR	**GOOD**	**EXCELLENT**

   a. 3
   b. 6
   c. 9

Strange Creatures Found in the Sea

In 1979, an unusual form of life was discovered in the Pacific Ocean, near Venezuela.

Strange red worms have been found living in the sea at depths of more than 3 kilometers. The sea is very dark at those depths, and the warm water is heated by hot metals, such as zinc, iron, and copper, which bubble up from beneath the seafloor.

Scientists found the red worms by chance during exploratory trips made in the tiny submersible *Alvin*. According to biologists, these red worms are unlike other worms in several ways.

The red worms can grow to be as long as 2 or 3 meters. They live in long tubes that are as tough and flexible as strong plastic. Just as other sea animals make their own protective shells, the red worms make their tube "homes."

The worm feeds through the feathery end of its body. Its food is bacteria that it sifts from the water. The bacteria are nourishing because they feed on thick layers of minerals found on the ocean floor.

The body of the sea worm is red because its blood contains a large amount of *hemoglobin* (hē′mə glō′-bĭn). Hemoglobin carries oxygen to cells in the body and is the same chemical that makes blood red. The worm takes in oxygen from the surrounding seawater. Like most living things, the worm would die without oxygen.

The scientists brought back several giant worms for more study. One thing they need now is a new name for the red worm. The scientists like *Vestimentifera*. What do *you* think?

1. Hemoglobin is a chemical that carries _____ to cells in the body.

2. How does the red worm get its food?
    a. through a long tube
    b. through the feathery end of its body
    c. from the shells of other sea animals

3. The water in which the worms live is warmed by hot
    a. chemicals.   b. metals.   c. bacteria.

4. You can tell from the story that the red worms found by the scientists
    a. do not need sunlight to live.
    b. are very similar to other worms.
    c. have very little hemoglobin in their bodies.

5. How are the red worms and most other living things alike?
    a. Both must eat chemicals in order to survive.
    b. Both must have oxygen to live.
    c. Both need protective shells or coverings.

6. The zinc, iron, and copper found bubbling up from beneath the seafloor would come under the heading of
    a. Minerals.
    b. Metals.
    c. Chemicals.

7. If you tried to bend the tubes in which the worms live, the tubes would most likely
    a. bend without breaking.
    b. snap in two like long, hard sticks.
    c. remain rigid and not bend in any direction.

8. Fill in the missing link in the food chain below.

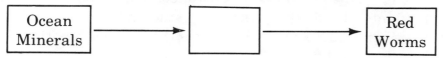

What's for Lunch?

The better you eat, the better you feel.

What is good food? That question is on the minds of many experts who study food to see if it is healthful, or *nutritious* (noo trĭsh'əs). These food experts, or nutritionists, are concerned about school lunches.

We eat about one-third of our daily food requirements at lunch. And the food we eat should help us grow and develop properly. So food experts are studying lunches to see if they contain the *nutrients* (noo'trē ənts) necessary for a healthy, well-balanced meal. Nutrients are the parts of a food that are used by our bodies for growth and energy. Proteins, fats, carbohydrates, vitamins, and minerals are nutrients.

Different foods contain varying amounts of nutrients. Foods that are high in calories supply the body with energy. Protein is used by the body to build new cells. Vitamin D—found in milk products—keeps bones healthy, while niacin helps us to grow. Certain minerals, such as iron, move oxygen through the body.

Nutritionists are constantly using new information about health and foods to help people plan nutritious meals. For example, nutritionists have learned that too much fat, sugar, or salt is not healthy. School dietitians keep this information in mind when planning lunch menus. But they known that even a well-balanced meal will not nourish the student who does not eat it. So school dietitians are adding nutrients to students' favorites, such as pizza, tacos, and milk shakes. Nutritionists feel that teaching students about nutrition encourages them to eat healthful foods.

1. The word in the story that means the same as *nutritious* is
    _____.

2. According to the story, nutrients are substances that are found
    in _____.

3. To make sure that the meals you eat are well balanced, it is
    important to
    a. eat a variety of foods.
    b. add up the number of calories in each meal.
    c. choose foods that are especially rich in protein.

4. The *main idea* of this story is that
    a. too much salt is not healthy.
    b. nutritionists plan well-balanced meals.
    c. what we eat has an important effect on our health.

*To answers questions 5, 6, 7, and 8, complete the following chart
using information from the story.*

SOME NUTRIENTS AND
THEIR EFFECT ON YOUR BODY

Nutrient	What It Does
Protein	Builds new _____ 5
_____ 6	Keeps bones healthy
_____ 7	Moves oxygen through the body
Niacin	Helps our bodies _____ 8

Underwater Geniuses

As far back as 300 B.C., humans have been fascinated by those playful sea mammals that can "speak."

The Greek scientist Aristotle was the first to report that dolphins could speak. But it is only recently that humans have begun to study closely the habits of the dolphins. Dolphins are considered to be highly intelligent animals with well-developed brains. Perhaps the dolphins' most fascinating characteristic is their use of sound to communicate with each other.

Dolphins employ two distinct sound systems: *echolocation* (ĕk′ō lō kā′shən) and "dolphin language." Echolocation is the ability to use high-frequency sounds to locate living and nonliving things. Dolphins use echolocation by sending out clicking sounds that bounce off underwater objects and return as echoes. The echoes give the dolphins clues to the shape, size, distance, and other characteristics of these objects.

Although dolphins have no vocal cords, they can emit whistles, squeaks, and groans. This second sound system, called dolphin language, is more complex and less understood than echolocation. However, research shows that at least some sounds made by dolphins, such as cries for help, are a form of language. Some scientists believe that dolphins can communicate complicated information. It seems, for example, that they are able to warn other dolphins to avoid fishnets.

Scientists are eager to understand more about dolphin language so that they can communicate with trained dolphins. If this communication is possible, dolphins might be sent on rescue missions to aid humans as well as underwater life. And some people think dolphins will be willing and able to help.

1. The dolphin's ability to locate objects by using sound is calle _____ .

2. Who first reported that dolphins could speak?

3. Dolphins are considered to be most interesting because of their ability to
   - a. play tricks.   b. hear human sounds.
   - c. use sound to communicate.

4. Before a dolphin can understand and interpret a click, the sound must
   - a. come back in the form of an echo.   b. pass through a bar-shaped object.   c. be sent to other dolphins nearby.

5. A dolphin's ability to emit squeaks, whistles, and groans is considered very unusual because a dolphin
   - a. is a sea mammal.   b. has no vocal cords.
   - c. does not have a highly developed brain.

Use the table to answer questions 6, 7, and 8.

SCIENTISTS WHO STUDY DOLPHINS

Name	Occupation	Special Interest
Kenneth S. Norris	Biologist	Echolocation intelligence
Sylvia D. Earle	Marine biologist	Marine animals
John Cunningham Lilly	Neurophysiologist	Dolphin language intelligence
Louis Millerman	Psychologist	Dolphin language memory

6. According to the table, which scientist studies sea animals other than the dolphin?

7. Which two scientists would be especially interested in understanding a dolphin's whistles, squeaks, and groans?

8. Kenneth S. Norris probably has a good understanding of how dolphins can
   - a. speak without vocal cords.   b. distinguish between objects.
   - c. help humans with work.

The Bee Team

It's not easy to fool a bee.

A honeybee colony may contain as many as 30,000 to 40,000 bees. They survive the winter by clustering together in a dense ball. The safety and well-being of the hive depend on the bees' efficient teamwork.

Behavioral (bĭ hāv′yər əl) scientists study how humans and animals behave. They believe that honeybees act in a very organized way. A bee may accidentally *pollinate* (pŏl′ə nāt′), or fertilize, flowers while gathering nectar, a sweet liquid used by bees to make honey. But behavioral scientists belive that the finding and gathering of nectar is an organized and skillful process.

Recently, studies have been done on the bee's ability to "map" a route and "observe" geogrpahy. While a scout bee hunts for flowers, it keeps track of the sun, shadows, and any outstanding land features. Once it has found new sources of nectar, the bee makes a beeline for home, flying directly to a landmark, such as a tree or a rock, near the hive. Upon returning, the bee communicates its discovery to other bees through a dance. The nectar gatherers are then able to fly directly to the flower. Somehow, the scout bee has described the route, or path, to the nectar.

Behavioral scientists have done one study in which a sugar syrup is placed near a hive. Scout bees quickly locate the syrup and "spread the word." But every few minutes, the scientists move the sugar 25 percent farther away from the hive. Soon, the bees catch on to this pattern and fly directly to the site. Once again, honeybees prove that they cannot easily be fooled.

1. In the story, *pollinate* means the same as _____.

2. Behavioral scientists study the behavior of
    a. humans and flowers.
    b. animals and humans.
    c. bees only.

3. The safety and well-being of the hive depend on
    a. how many flowers are pollinated.
    b. the bees' working together as a team.
    c. where the bees wander.

4. In the story, the term *beeline* is used to describe how a bee
    a. observes the geography of a place.
    b. heads for a landmark near its hive.
    c. hunts for new patches of flowers.

5. Which of the following statements is true?
    a. Honeybees are not able to survive cold temperatures.
    b. Scout bees have the ability to map routes.
    c. Bees can be tricked by changing the location of the nectar.

Worker bees perform several jobs. To answer questions 6, 7, and 8, put the number of the bees' job description on the line in front of the similar job done by humans.

6. feeding newborn bees   _____ guards

7. protecting the hive from enemies   _____ nurses

8. cleaning empty cells in the hive for reuse   _____ house workers

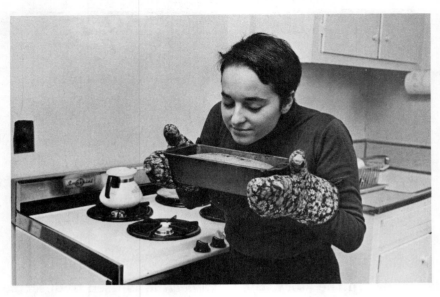

Their Noses
Know Not What
They Smell

Although our sense of smell is 10,000 times more sensitive than any of our other senses, it is usually taken for granted.

Most of us enjoy the odor of freshly baked bread, hot buttered popcorn, or sizzling bacon. But, to some people, the odors of fresh bread, burning rubber, and pizza are all the same. These people suffer from a condition called *anosmia* (ăn ŏz′mē ə). They have lost their sense of smell.

A normal sense of smell can provide information about distant objects. We do not have to be in the kitchen to know that the toast is burning. And we don't have to see a puddle to know that a gas tank is leaking. But people with anosmia are not warned of such unseen dangers.

A condition called *phantosmia* (fănt ŏz′mē ə) causes people to smell odors that are not there—phantom odors. Seated at dinner, such a person may

be sickened by the odor of a bowl of soup. Others at the table think that the same soup smells delicious. But the person with phantosmia smells something very different and may become quite ill.

Smell is a chemical sense, which means that it is triggered by chemicals in the things we smell. Scientists have several theories to explain why this is so.

One theory is based on the vibration, or movement, of the atoms in the molecules of things we smell. For example, if the chemicals in different objects have the same vibrations, the objects give off the same odor. According to another theory, if the molecules in things we smell have the same shape, the things will give off the same odor.

At this time, neither theory has been proved. Who knows what the nose knows?

1. People who suffer from a condition called _____ have lost their sense of smell.

2. People who smell odors that are not there suffer from a condition called _____.

3. According to the story, the sense of smell is triggered by _____ in the things we smell.

4. It is not necessary to see something in order to smell it.
   a. True
   b. False
   c. The story does not say.

5. According to one theory in the story, if two different foods smell the same, then it is possible that
   a. their chemicals have the same vibrations.
   b. they were cooked in the same chemical substance.
   c. they contain the same chemical ingredients

6. Besides smell, the sense of _____ also gives us information about distant objects.
   a. taste   b. touch   c. hearing

7. Besides smell, the sense of _____ is also a chemical sense.
   a. sight
   b. taste
   c. touch

8. Match each sense in Column I with the part of the body in which it is found in Column II.

Column I	Column II
a. touch	____ nose
b. taste	____ eyes
c. smell	____ skin
d. hearing	____ ears
e. sight	____ tongue

Insects Beware— A Dragonfly Is Near!

Some 400 different kinds of dragonflies live on or near the water in the United States.

Dragonflies fly swiftly from place to place, sometimes darting so quickly that they are difficult to see. They have 2 sets of wings that range from 5 to 13 centimeters long.

A dragonfly is considered to be one of the most beneficial, or helpful, insects to have around because it is a predator. A predator is an animal that preys on, or kills, other animals. The dragonfly is beneficial to humans because it eats other insects that humans consider to be pests. To catch the insects, the dragonfly puts its legs together and curves them so that they form a "basket." Then, it uses this basket to scoop up insects from the air.

Dragonflies have an interesting life history. They lay their eggs under-water. The young hatch in about 3 weeks and are called *nymphs* (nĭmfs). Nymphs have no wings. They *molt* (mōlt), or shed their skins, as often as 10 to 15 times as they continue to live underwater. To survive, they prey on small underwater animals. It takes from 1 to 4 years before the last nymph stage is reached, and the nymph crawls out of the water. Then it splits its skin, and a winged adult dragonfly comes out.

After its wings dry, the dragonfly begins its role as a beneficial predator, preying on such insects as mosquitoes and flies. Sometimes, the dragonfly will eat insects that are considered beneficial to humans. But that is because all insects look like food to the hungry dragonfly!

1. The newly hatched young of the dragonfly are called
    _____.

2. Dragonflies help humans by eating _____.

3. Where does the dragonfly lay its eggs?
    a. in the sand
    b. on leaves
    c. in the water

4. You can tell when the dragonfly is attacking an insect because
    its
    a. wings flap up and down.
    b. skin splits open.
    c. legs curve to form a basket.

5. Before the dragonfly can become a predator, it must *first*
    _____ its wings.
    a. shed   b. dry   c. open

6. Which of the following statements *best* expresses the main idea
    of the story?
    a. To humans, the dragonfly is a beneficial predator.
    b. The dragonfly is one of our most annoying pests.
    c. The life history of the dragonfly is very interesting.

7. How would you rate a mosquito's ability to escape the
    dragonfly?

1 2 3	4 5 6 7	8 9 10
FAIR	**VERY GOOD**	**EXCELLENT**

    a. 3   b. 7   c. 10

8. Under which of the following headings would you list the
    nymph?
    a. Choosy Eaters   b. Skin Shedders   c. Strong Flyers

Heart Care Starts Early

Establishing good health habits early in life may help prevent heart disease.

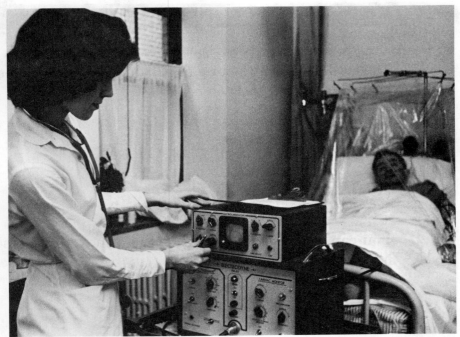

Due to research, most doctors now believe that it is important to care for your heart when you are young, before a problem can develop into something serious. By guarding against heart disease, you will ensure that your heart can do its job properly. The job of the heart is to pump blood to all parts of the body. Blood is carried away from the heart through blood vessels called *arteries* (är′ tə rēz) and is returned to the heart through blood vessels called *veins* (vānz).

Many things can strain your heart and result in heart disease. Heart disease includes any condition that can weaken the heart or interfere with the way this marvelous circulatory system works. The most common problem is called hardening of the arteries. It occurs when deposits of a fatty substance called *cholesterol* (kə lĕs′ tə rôl′) collect slowly inside the walls of the arteries. As the cholesterol builds up, the openings of the arteries get narrow and the walls of the arteries begin to harden. The heart must work harder to move the blood through the narrowed arteries.

Overweight is another common problem. Overweight strains the heart because the heart must pump blood to the extra body fat. When blood flows through the blood vessels with too much force, high blood pressure, or hypertension, can result. Hypertension causes stress and strain on your heart. Doctors now also think that eating too much salt often causes hypertension.

So be good to your heart. Avoid beef, butter, cheese, and other foods that are high in cholesterol and fat content. Reduce your intake of salt, and keep your weight down by eating sensibly and exercising regularly.

Use the terms below to answer questions 1 through 3.

    veins   arteries   cholesterol   hypertension

1. A fatty substance present in many foods is called _____.

2. Blood travels to the heart through vessels called _____.

3. Too much salt in the diet may cause _____.

4. What effect does hardening of the arteries have on the heart?
   a. Blood flows to the heart with too much force.
   b. The heart works harder to pump blood.
   c. It is difficult for the heart to pump blood to extra body fat.

5. Which of the following statements is *true*?
   a. Overweight is the most common problem that leads to heart disease.
   b. Eating fatty foods may cause hardening of the arteries.
   c. Guarding against heart disease requires the help of a doctor.

6. Of the following, which would be the *best* food to avoid if you wanted to cut down on high-cholesterol foods?
   a. steak   b. chicken   c. fish

Use the diagram to answer questions 7 and 8.

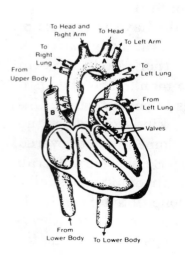

7. What type of blood vessel is labeled "A" in the diagram?

8. What type of blood vessel is labeled "B" in the diagram?

At Home in a Coconut Shell

Did you ever see a shell walking?

Hermit crabs live on land, in shallow water, or at great depths in the oceans. They can live in both cold-water and warm-water regions. One kind of crab, the land hermit crab, lives in the Florida Keys.

Land hermit crabs lay their eggs in water. After the young hatch, they spend the first part of their lives in water.

The rest of their lives is spent on land, but they always stay near water. Land hermit crabs eat both plant and animal food and will often climb high trees in search of food.

All hermit crabs have five pairs of legs and three main body parts—a *head,* a *thorax* (thôr′ ăks′), and an *abdomen* (ăb′ də mən). The abdomen is soft and needs to be protected. Unlike some other kinds of crabs, the hermit crab's abdomen is not covered by a hard shell. So the hermit crab makes its home in empty seashells, where it lives alone, like a hermit. It twists itself into a curved shell, leaving some of its legs sticking out for *locomotion* (lō′kə mō′shən). (Locomotion is the ability to move from place to place.)

The crab's first pair of legs are *chelipeds* (kē′lə pĕdz)—that is, they have claws. The right cheliped is larger than the left one. The chelipeds are used for defense and for capturing food. After the hermit crab withdraws into its shell, it uses its right cheliped to block the shell's entrance.

As the crab grows, it begins to outgrow its protective shell and must look for a new home. The hermit crab sometimes kills a snail or another crab to steal its shell. If it can not find a suitable new shell, the hermit crab may use things such as broken coconut shells and old plastic baby bottles for its home.

1. The ability to move from place to place is called _____

2. Where do land hermit crabs lay their eggs?
   a. in trees   b. in water   c. on land

3. Why is it necessary for hermit crabs to seek new homes?
   a. They grow too large for their old shells.
   b. They must change their hiding places.
   c. They need new homes when they move to land.

4. Why is the crab in this story called a hermit?
   a. because it can climb trees   b. because it eats animal food
   c. because it lives alone

5. Which of the following would be the *best* nickname for the hermit crab?
   a. The Shy Crab   b. The Robber Crab   c. The Baby Crab

6. Which of the following would offer the *most* protection for a land hermit crab?
   a. an old shoe   b. a torn rag   c. a leaf

Use the diagram to answer questions 7 and 8.

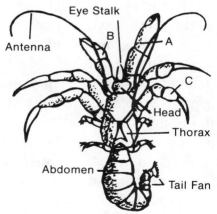

7. To block the entrance to its shell, the hermit crab uses the part of its body that is labeled _____ on the diagram.
   a. A   b. B   c. C

8. The first part of the hermit crab's body to enter the shell is called the
   a. Antenna.   b. Tail Fan.   c. Abdomen.

Meet the Mushroom

What kind of plant does not have seeds, roots, or green leaves? It's the mushroom.

Mushrooms belong to a plant group called *fungi* (fŭn′jē). Mushrooms can be as beautiful and as colorful as wild flowers. Mushrooms do not have leaves or seeds and, unlike green plants, they cannot make their own food. Since they need a lot of moisture, mushrooms usually grow where it is damp. They may be found growing in decaying leaves, twigs, and stumps as well as in rich soil and on living trees.

The main part of the mushroom grows underground and is called the *mycelium* (mī sē′lē əm). The mycelium is the mass of thread-like, branching strands that forms the main part of a fungus. When the mushroom grows on a living tree, the mycelium causes the tree to decay. This decay is a source of food for the mushroom. The umbrella-like growth is a stalk that grows up from the mycelium. This stalk is really the fruit of the mushroom. The top of the "umbrella" is the cap. On the underside of the cap are the gills, from which the spores of the plant develop.

Mushrooms and other fungi make spores instead of seeds. When the fruit is ripe, the spores fall to the ground or are scattered by the wind. Some of the spores sprout, and a new mushroom plant develops. Spores can be white, yellow, pink, black, or brown. Their color helps identify those plants that are safe to eat. Only about 1,000 of the more than 38,000 kinds of wild mushrooms are safe to eat. The common table mushroom is grown in special mushroom houses and is safe and tasty to eat.

1. The mass of thread-like, branching strands that forms the main part of the mushroom is called the _____.

2. Mushrooms belong to a plant group called _____.

3. Unlike green plants, mushrooms cannot
   a. make their own food.
   b. grow in damp, wet places.
   c. be eaten.

4. According to the story, one way of distinguishing a safe mushroom from a poisonous one is by the
   a. size of its stalk.
   b. color of its spores.
   c. shape of its gills.

5. This story also might have been called
   a. "Growing Mushrooms."
   b. "All About the Mushroom Plant."
   c. "Plants That Are Safe to Eat."

Use the diagram below to answer questions 6, 7, and 8.

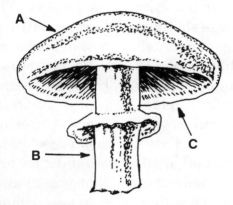

6. The parts of the mushroom from which the spores develop are labeled _____ and are called the _____.

7. The part of the mushroom called the cap is labeled _____.

8. The fruit of the mushroom is labeled _____.

Life Under a Pier

Living things are continually moving around beneath piers.

A *pier* (pîr) is a platform that extends from a shore out over water and can be used as a landing place for boats or ships. Most piers are supported by heavy wooden pillars, or *pilings* (pī'lĭngz), that have been sunk into the seafloor.

There is a lot of activity going on around these underwater pilings. For example, it is not uncommon to find a piling covered with different kinds of sea animals, such as mussels, that live and feed at the water level. These shellfish attach themselves to pilings by tough "threads." By opening their shells to allow water to flow through, mussels are able to sift out tiny bits of plant and animal food from the water.

Starfish can also be found living near pilings, since they feed off shellfish, such as oysters and mussels, that have attached themselves to a piling. Starfish use their arms to pry open oyster and mussel shells. Then, the starfish can easily extend their stomachs inside the shells to feed on the bodies of the shellfish.

Barnacles, anemones, sponges, and sea urchins also attach themselves to the pilings. They, in turn, attract fish that swim in and around the pilings looking for a meal.

People often toss trash off piers, littering the seafloor. In this litter, living things are moving around in search of food or a home. For example, octopuses can be seen swimming around. The octopus is a sea creature that makes good use of litter. For an octopus, "Home Sweet Home" may be an old tin can!

48

1. The wooden supports that hold up a pier are called pillars, or _____.

2. One function of a pier is to serve as a _____ for ships.

3. What do mussels use to attach themselves to piers?

4. What must a mussel do in order to obtain food?
   a. stick out its stomach
   b. open its shell
   c. attach itself to a plant

5. According to the story, what is the enemy of mussels and oysters?
   a. the sponge
   b. the sea urchin
   c. the starfish

6. Of the following, for what purpose might an octopus use litter?
   a. to make its home
   b. to sift out food
   c. to float around on

7. The activity that goes on around a piling results in a kind of _____.
   a. food chain
   b. hiding place
   c. shoreline

8. Fill in the following diagram:

	Mussels	Starfish

   a. Barnacles
   b. Tiny bits of plants and animals
   c. Octopuses

Measuring Up to Sports

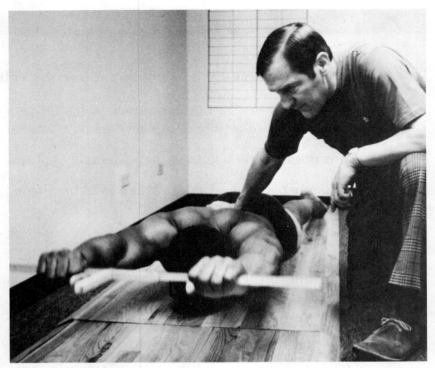

Doctors use tape measures and computers to check sports stars.

The person at bat has thick, heavy bones and large muscles. The batter has big arms and wrists and very long legs. This athlete is perfectly built for hitting a baseball over the fence. Who says so? Dr. Marvin I. Clein says so. Dr. Clein is a muscle specialist. He can tell you just which muscles are important for which sports.

Athletes from all over the country come to Dr. Clein's laboratory in Denver, Colorado for testing. First, Dr. Clein takes the person's measurements to answer some important questions. How tall is this person? Which is longer, the upper or lower arm? How far can the fingers stretch?

Then, Dr. Clein does other tests to find out how strong the muscles are. He also determines how well the person's body uses oxygen. Efficient use of oxygen is necessary for changing food into energy.

All the information is then analyzed by a computer. When this electronic device, or machine, is fed information about a person's body, it returns answers like these:

—This athlete has long arms, hands, and fingers; a long trunk; and long lower legs. She would make a good baseball pitcher.

—This person has bowed legs, thick bones and muscles, and short upper legs. He could be a good tackler on a football team.

Having the right build and strength is not enough to guarantee doing well at a sport. The mind plays an important role, too. So Dr. Clein also does tests to find out if the athlete's state of mind will help the body to do well.

1. The electronic device used to analyze an athlete's test results is a _____ .

2. Besides the right build and strength, the _____ plays an important role in succeeding at sports.

3. According to the story, when an athlete comes to the laboratory, what does Dr. Clein do *first?*
   a. He finds out how strong the athlete is.
   b. He takes the athlete's measurements.
   c. He checks the athlete's use of oxygen.

4. The doctor in the story *must* have a very good understanding of _____ to do his job.
   a. muscles   b. tests   c. computers

Use the chart to answer Questions 5, 6, 7, and 8.

PHYSICAL SKILLS AND SOME SPORTS AND ACTIVITIES IN WHICH THEY ARE USED		
Physical Skill	**What It Means**	**Some Sports and Activities**
Agility	Being able to move easily and smoothly when bending, twisting, or stretching	Ballet, diving, judo, skateboarding, soccer, volleyball, yoga
Coordination	Being able to use smoothly a number of muscles at one time to complete a certain task.	Ballet, baseball, basketball, golf, hockey, softball, swimming, tennis
Endurance	Being able to perform a physical task for long periods of time (Almost all activities require some endurance.)	Ballet, bicycling, boxing, football, hiking, jogging, skiing, tennis, track and field, wrestling
Equilibrium	Being able to balance yourself easily if your body begins to sway or lean in one direction	Ballet, bowling, fencing, gymnastics hockey, horseback riding, skateboarding, yoga
Speed	Being able to move the parts of your body fast	Ballet, baseball, ice skating, handball, softball, tennis

5. Which sport or activity requires the use of *all* the physical skills listed on the chart?

6. Which physical skill do you possess if you are able to perform a sport or activity for long periods of time?

7. According to the chart, one of the physical skills you need to play basketball is _____ .

8. Besides agility, what other skill does a skateboarder need?

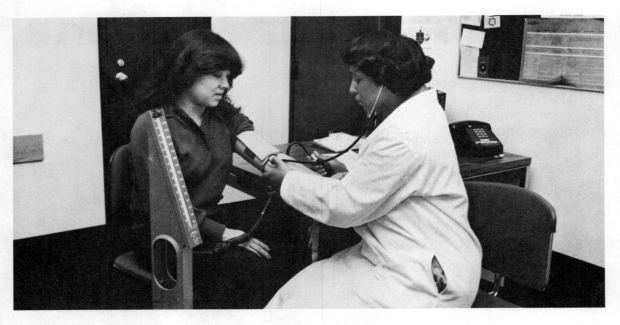

Watch the Salt!

How much salt is enough?

We have all seen people use a salt-shaker so vigorously that they practically cover the plate with salt. Sometimes they salt the food even before tasting it. But oversalting is not a good idea, because salt is thought to be dangerous for many people.

There is a lot of evidence that salt is a factor in causing high blood pressure, or hypertension. The sodium in table salt, or sodium chloride, holds water in the body. This makes it harder for a person's circulatory system to work properly and increases his or her blood pressure.

We do not know why some people get hypertension and others do not. One theory suggests that large amounts of salt taken in daily from childhood on can trigger hypertension in adults. Other possible causes of hypertension may include heredity, psychological factors, physical condition, and diet.

Although salt is essential to life, nutrition experts recommend that we control the amount of salt in our diet. Most of us could do very nicely with about 2 grams of salt a day. We can get this amount from our food without using additional salt. For example, a hot dog or a dill pickle has the same amount of sodium as 5 grams of salt.

About 30 million people in the United States are good candidates for high blood pressure. If someone in your family suffers from this condition, your own risk of getting hypertension is higher than normal. Think about watching *your* salt intake *now*.

1. In the story, the word that means "high blood pressure" is _____ .

2. Another term for table salt is _____ .

3. Nutrition experts tell us that most people should _____ salt in their diets.
   a. increase the use of
   b. control the amount of
   c. stop using any

4. The story suggests that a low-sodium diet would be _____ for persons with high blood pressure.
   a. good   b. dangerous   c. useless

5. Today, doctors know how and why people get high blood pressure.
   a. True   b. False   c. The story does not say.

6. High blood pressure may begin at an early age. Therefore, it would be a good idea to
   a. have your blood pressure checked from childhood on.
   b. eat only between 5 and 6 grams of salt a day.
   c. stop eating any form of salt.

7. Fill in the missing link in the chain of events below.

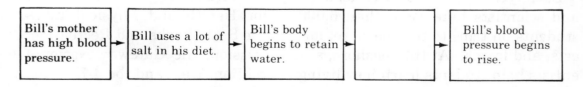

8. In the chain of events above, why would Bill's chances of having high blood pressure be greater than someone else's, even though the other person also uses a lot of salt?

Operation Explore—People Working Together

Explore the seashore. Visit a farm. Walk through a forest. Is it possible to do these things if you live in a large city? Yes, it is, if you belong to a special program called Operation Explore in New York City.

Operation Explore was started by people in New York who wanted to give students the opportunity to explore the various environments that surround their city.

Each year, teachers, 4-H leaders, and scientists take more than 5,000 students on trips to the seashore, forests, and farms. At the seashore, scientists help students learn how living things depend on each other. The students collect some of the sea animals, place them in saltwater tanks, and bring them back to their classrooms. The sea animals are then placed in saltwater aquariums for further study.

In the forest, students walk along special trails and observe how different plants and animals live together. They also learn how forest plants and animals depend on each other. On the farm, students try out farm tools and learn how farm animals are raised and how food is grown.

Operation Explore is successful because of the work of many people from the following organizations: Cornell University, New York City's Center for Health and Physical Education, the State Parks and Recreation Commission, the Gateway National Recreation Area, and the 4-H Club in the city. These people have enriched the students' understanding of their environment and have shown what good things can happen when people work together.

A Visit to the Dallas Health and Science Museum

One of the most interesting attractions in Texas is the Dallas Health and Science Museum. Thousands of people visit the museum every year.

There are many exhibits to see. One exhibit is a giant model of the human eye. It is 60 times the size of the normal eye. Visitors can learn how the human eye works and how to take care of it. Other models in the museum include a transparent man and woman and a popular exhibit called the Birth of a Baby.

In addition to exhibits on health and medicine, the museum has a planetarium. A planetarium is a special device, or machine, that shows reproductions of stars, moons, and planets on the inside surface of a rounded dome. During one of the shows, called "The Magic of Mars," scientists explain the movement of planets and stars in the Milky Way Galaxy. There is also a special show for Dallas girl scouts, boy scouts, and campfire girls. The show is called "Scouting with the Stars," and it was planned to help the scouts earn merit badges, star badges, and science honors.

There is a preschool section at the museum where children can study about different countries. In the picture above, a youngster is learning about Japan. She is being shown how to use chopsticks.

The Dallas Health and Science Museum also has a special program called Summer Search during the summer months. During this time, children can study astronomy, art, nutrition, chemistry, and puppetry.

Mammals of North America

Fill in the spaces with the names of the North American mammals listed below.

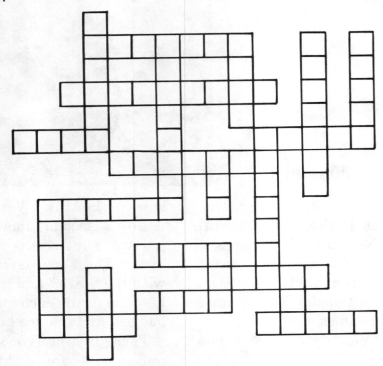

3-Letter Words

elk
bat
fox

4-Letter Words

mole
mink
lynx
bear
seal
wolf

5-Letter Words

otter
moose
whale
skunk

6-Letter Words

walrus
weasel
coyote

7-Letter Words

caribou
raccoon
muskrat
opossum

8-Letter Word

squirrel

9-Letter Word

porcupine

The Spiral

Help the bee find the rose. Stay inside the tube, and crawl quickly to the flower. Hurry! The bee has lots of work to do.

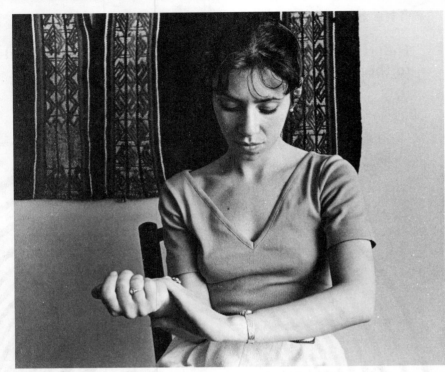

Investigating Your Heartbeat Rate

How many times does your heart beat in a minute? How do exercise and other activities change your heartbeat rate? There are places on your body that tell how fast your heart is beating. These places are called pulse points. One pulse point is on your inner wrist, below your thumb. Others are on your neck, beneath your ears. Find a pulse point on your body. Count the number of beats in 20 seconds. Multiply by 3. This is your pulse rate, or the number of times your heart beats per minute.

Compare your pulse rates with those of your classmates. Record the pulse rates on a chart like the one below. Discuss your findings.

NUMBER OF HEARTBEATS PER MINUTE

LYING DOWN—RELAXED	
SITTING DOWN—RELAXED	
AFTER A MINUTE OF JOGGING IN PLACE	
AFTER EATING	

How Many Beats in a Lifetime?

The shrew is a tiny animal—smaller than a mouse. A shrew's heart beats about 1,000 times per minute. A shrew will live for about 1 year. A shrew's heart beats 525,600,000 times in its lifetime. Here is how we can figure this out.

1,000 beats per minute × 60 = 60,000 beats per hour
60,000 beats per hour × 24 = 1,440,000 beats per day
1,440,000 beats per day × 365 = 525,600,000 beats per year

Figure out how many heartbeats there are in the lifetime of these animals. Use a calculator to do the math. Record your findings on a chart like the one below.

	HEARTBEAT RATE PER MINUTE	LIFE EXPECTANCY (in years)	HEARTBEATS IN A LIFETIME (in billions)
SHREW	1,000	1	0.526
MOUSE	550	2	0.578
RAT	450	3	0.709
RABBIT	160	6	0.505
PIG	80	8	0.336
SHEEP	75	9	0.335
COW	60	10	0.315
LION	45	13	0.307
HORSE	40	22	0.463
ELEPHANT	30	35	0.552
WHALE	17	70	0.625
HUMAN	72	75	2.840

Look at the chart. From shrew to whale, the highest number of lifetime heartbeats is _____ billion. There are nearly _____ billion heartbeats in a human lifetime. What reasons might account for this difference?

Investigating Your Senses

In this science adventure, you are invited to learn about three of your senses. They are touch, taste, and sight.

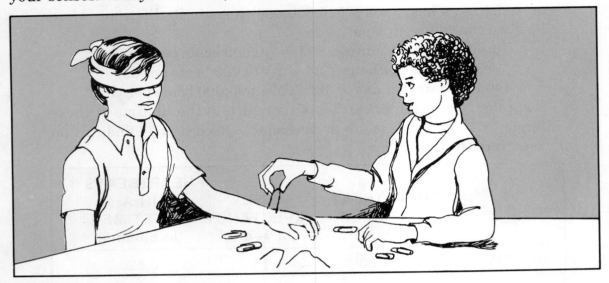

Touch

Suppose you wanted to find out about something by touching it. Would you use your fingertips or your elbow? Maybe that sounds like a silly question. But why would you use your fingertips? Is it just because of where they are located? Or is there more than that involved? Could it be that fingertips are better "feelers" than other parts of your body? There are more nerve endings in your fingertips than anywhere else. Try the following activity to learn about these nerve endings.

Bend five paper clips into U shapes. Make the open ends of the first clip 1 centimeter wide. Make the open ends of the second clip 2 centimeters wide. Continue the same way. The open ends of the last clip will be 5 centimeters apart. Ask someone to touch both ends of each U clip to different parts of your body. Start with the 5-centimeter U. Can you feel both ends of the clip? Now try the 4-centimeter clip. Do you still feel both ends? Continue with each remaining clip. Can you feel the 1-centimeter U? If so, many nerve endings are in the part touched. Tell the person you are working with to fool you. This can be done by sometimes touching you with only one point. Which areas of your body are the most sensitive to touch? These have the most nerve endings.

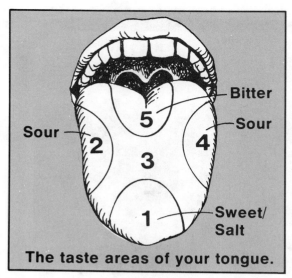

Sour

Bitter

Sour

5

2

4

3

1

Sweet/ Salt

The taste areas of your tongue.

Taste

Located on your tongue are tiny taste buds. When you taste something, they are at work. The diagram shows where the basic sets of taste buds are.

Test each of these areas with different foods and liquids. Try orange juice, milk, vinegar, onion juice, and pickle juice. Also use sugar, salt, apple, potato, lemon, and unsweetened chocolate. Each test can be done by a friend. Have your friend dip the end of a toothpick into each substance. Then ask him or her to touch different areas on your tongue. Keep a record of what you observe. Rinse your mouth with water after each test. Can you taste sweet things better at the tip of your tongue? Can you taste bitter things better toward the back of your tongue? Where do you taste sour things best? Where do you taste salty things best?

Sight

Your eyes focus by themselves on things near and far. But how close an object can your eyes focus on? Use a book and a meter stick. Hold them as the girl in the picture is doing. Move the book in and out until the print is clearly in focus. Do it 3 times, and record the distance each time. Then, average your results. Compare your focusing distance with those of your classmates. What do you find out for persons who wear glasses? Is their focusing distance the same with and without glasses?

EARTH-SPACE SCIENCE

The earth's crust is a storehouse of materials that are of interest to many different kinds of scientists. Paleontologists search for fossils in order to discover what kinds of plants and animals lived during various periods of the earth's history. Archaeologists uncover ancient tools, buildings, and other objects to learn how people lived in the distant past. Mineralogists identify and study the minerals found in the earth, and petroleum geologists explore for deposits of oil and gas.

Halley's Comet

Bright comets are spectacular sights, but they are not often seen by the human eye.

In 1682, the English astronomer Edmund Halley identified and studied the motion of a bright comet. First, he figured out the comet's *orbit* (ôr'bĭt), or path, around the sun. Then, Halley studied the records of two bright comets observed in 1531 and 1607. He decided that all three were actually the same comet returning to Earth's view about every 76 years. Based on these studies, Halley predicted that the comet would reappear in 1758. His prediction was right, and on December 24, 1758, the comet returned. Since then, every 76 years the comet, now called Halley's comet, comes close enough to Earth to be seen either through a telescope or by the naked eye.

The main part of a comet is its *nucleus* (nōo'klē əs). The nucleus is made up of frozen water, methane, and other gases. Billions of tiny pieces of rock are frozen into the "ice." As you can see in the diagram on the next page, a comet can be very near the sun at one point in its orbit and very far away at another point. As the comet comes closer to the sun, the icy material of its nucleus starts to melt and evaporate. A tail of gas and rock particles forms and may stream millions of kilometers into space.

Solar winds cause the bright, glowing tail to always point away from the sun. A comet's tail is longest when it is nearest the sun. As it moves farther away from the sun, the tail gets smaller and smaller until it finally disappears.

When it appeared in 1910, Halley's comet could be seen clearly in the sky. When the comet appeared in 1985/86, it was farther from the Earth. Light pollution from Earth dimmed some of the comet's light. But it could still be seen without a telescope.

Use the word list below to answer questions 1, 2, and 3.

nucleus   orbit   telescope

1. A comet's path around the sun is also called its _____.

2. The main part of a comet is its _____.

3. An instrument that makes far away objects easier to see is called a _____.

4. The first recorded sighting of Halley's comet was in the year _____.

5. What causes a comet's tail to form?
    a. solar winds,
    b. solar heat
    c. solar ice

6. After its appearance in 1986, Halley's comet will return again in the year _____.

The orbit of Halley's comet is shown in blue in the diagram below. Use the diagram to answer questions 7 and 8.

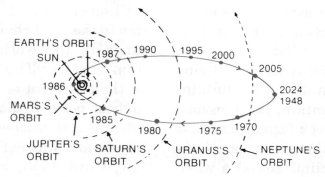

7. The year before it approaches Earth's orbit in 1986, Halley's comet will be just outside the orbit of
    a. Saturn.   b. Jupiter.   c. Mars.

8. When will Halley's comet be in the same place as it was in 1948?

Conquering the World's Peaks

Why would anyone want to climb a mountain?

During the 1700s, scientists began asking questions about the structure and origin of mountains. To find the answers to these questions, they *ascended* (ə sĕnd′ĕd), or climbed, some of the world's most interesting mountains.

Many of the early ascents were made in the French, Swiss, and Italian Alps. The Swiss scientist De Saussure made one of the first successful climbs of Mont Blanc, a Swiss mountain. While on the mountain, De Saussure studied glaciers, rock formations, and high-altitude weather patterns. News of De Saussure's climb set off a wave of interest in mountain climbing throughout Europe. Soon, not only other scientists but pure adventurers began to climb mountains.

From the late 1700s through the 1800s, many famous mountains were climbed for the first time. Among these were the Matterhorn in Switzerland, Kilimanjaro in Africa, Mount Whitney in California, and Mount McKinley in Alaska. The middle 1800s became known as the "Golden Age of Mountain Climbing." During this time, the first mountain-climbing clubs were formed.

Climbers soon turned their attention to the most challenging mountain range in the world, the *Himalayas* (hĭm′ə lā′əz). This mountain range, on the continent of Asia, includes the highest peak on Earth, Mount Everest. Everest reaches 8708 meters into the air and was not ascended successfully until 1953, when Sir Edmund Hillary set foot on the summit. It has been climbed a number of times since then.

1. In the story, the word _____ means "climbed."

2. The Golden Age of Mountain Climbing occurred during the middle
        a. 1700s.   b. 1800s.   c. 1900s.

3. One of the first people to climb Mont Blanc successfully was _____ .

4. Besides climbing for scientific reasons, people also climbed mountains for adventure.
        a. True   b. False   c. The story does not say.

5. Sir Edmund Hillary made history by being the first person to
   a. form a mountain-climbing club.   b. climb to the top of Mount Everest.   c. study rock formations and glaciers.

Use the table to answer questions 6, 7, and 8.

HIGHEST AND LOWEST ALTITUDES ON THE SEVEN CONTINENTS

Continent	Highest Point	Meters Above Sea Level	Lowest Point	Meters Below Sea Level
Asia	Mount Everest, Nepal-Tibet	8708	Dead Sea, Israel-Jordan	391
South America	Aconcagua, Argentina	6850	Valdes Peninsula, Argentina	39
North America	Mount McKinley, Alaska	6096	Death Valley, California	85
Africa	Kilimanjaro, Tanzania	5802	Lake Assal, Djiboun	152
Europe	Mount Elbrus, U.S.S.R.	5553	Caspian Sea, U.S.S.R.	28
Antarctica	Vinson Massif	5058	—	—
Australia	Mount Kosciusko, New South Wales	2193	Lake Eyre, South Australia	16

6. The lowest mountain listed is on the continent of _____ .

7. Mount McKinley is ranked the _____ highest peak in the world.
        a. second   b. third   c. fourth

8. Which of the following is the lowest point in the world?
        a. Lake Eyre   b. Death Valley   c. the Dead Sea

Volcano Alert

The gray mushroom cloud rose nearly 8 kilometers into the sky.

On April 13, 1979, the residents of the Caribbean island of St. Vincent looked up in terror. They gazed fearfully at Soufrière, an island volcano, and Soufrière was erupting! Molten rock, or lava, and hot gases spouted out of this opening in the earth's crust. The eruption sounded like thunder rolling across the island. A gray, mushroom-shaped cloud rained ashes and cinders over a 60-kilometer area. People who lived in villages near the volcano fled for their lives.

Soufrière is an active volcano, that is, one that has erupted within the last 50 years or so. There are more than 500 active volcanoes in the world. A dormant volcano is one that is known to have erupted sometime during recorded human history. That is, someone actually witnessed the eruption and wrote about it. Extinct volcanoes are those that have not erupted within recorded time. But now and then, a supposedly extinct volcano, such as Lassen Peak in California, suddenly erupts.

Volcanologists, scientists who study volcanoes, use sensitive instruments to help them predict volcanic eruptions. Some volcanoes give warnings before they erupt. The ground near them begins to shake so slightly that the shaking cannot be felt by people. But the delicate instruments feel and record the shaking. When the volcanologists receive this information, they can tell that an eruption is about to take place. Then, people living near the volcano can be warned. With luck and speed, they will get away safely before the eruption.

1. A volcano that has erupted within the last 50 years or so is said to be _____.

2. According to the story, a volcano is actually an opening in the earth's _____.

3. When a volcano erupts, molten rock, or _____, and hot _____ pour out of the opening.

4. The instruments that scientists use to predict an eruption must be very sensitive to

       a. movement.   b. sound.   c. temperature.

5. An extinct volcano will never erupt again.

       a. True   b. False   c. The story does not say.

Use the chart below to answer questions 6, 7, and 8.

SOME MAJOR ERUPTIONS

Volcano	Location	Date of Eruption	Results
Krakatoa	Indonesia	1883	Over one-half of the island of Krakatoa was destroyed completely; great sea waves drowned 36,000 people on nearby islands; the explosion was felt more than 1600 kilometers away.
Mount Pelée	St. Pierre, Martinique (Caribbean island)	1902	There was a fiery explosion; gases and dust poured from the crater, smothering 30,000 people in St. Pierre and leaving 1 survivor.
Mount Usu	Japan	1977	Hot ashes poured from the crater; 20,000 tourists and 7,000 residents fled nearby towns; there was serious crop damage.

6. Which volcano would be considered active? On what date did it erupt?

7. The results show that the most violent eruption was located in _____.

8. Which volcano erupted with the result that people were smothered by gas and dust?

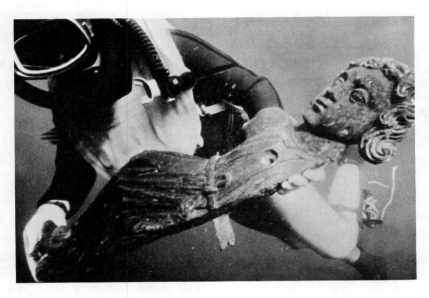

Sea Secrets

Are you hunting for the remains of an ancient city or a cargo of treasure? Try looking underwater.

In the 1600s, a Portuguese ship sank off the coast of Kenya. One of the objects recovered from the shipwreck can be seen in the picture above. As you can see, the 300-year-old wooden angel appears to be in fairly good condition.

Burial at sea slows down or even stops the normal processes of decay. Wood, cloth, and other fibers rot very slowly underwater as compared with above ground. Unlike things above ground, objects underwater are not subjected to the effects of wind, rain, and extreme changes in temperature.

Until recently, underwater exploration was an archaeologist's nightmare. But scuba-diving techniques and equipment now make it possible for divers to move around more freely, and wet suits protect them in cold waters. The development of underwater lights, cameras, and other equipment has also made the exploration easier.

However, underwater exploration is exhausting and often dangerous. It is also more time-consuming than working on land *digs*. (A *dig* is the term used to describe the place where archaeologists are working.) Divers usually work in pairs or small groups, and they can remain on the ocean bottom for only short periods of time. Then, they must return to the surface very slowly because of the change in water pressure as they rise. Rising too quickly could be fatal.

But the historical treasures raised from the deep are worth the effort. Archaeologists have found "drowned" villages from prehistoric times, flooded cities, and wrecked treasure ships. At last, the sea is giving up some of its secrets.

QUESTIONS

1. Places where archaeologists are working are known as
   _____ .

2. Special techniques and equipment allow divers to move around
   _____ underwater.

3. Underwater, the normal processes of decay
   a. are slower than they are above ground.
   b. destroy only wood and cloth objects.
   c. do not take place.

4. According to the story, what type of equipment enables divers
   to explore in cold-water areas?

5. Which of the following statements is *not* true of underwater
   exploration?
   a. Searches require a lot of time.
   b. Archaeologists work in small teams.
   c. Divers can work for long periods of time.

6. In recent years, techniques and equipment for underwater
   archaeology have been greatly
   a. improved.
   b. reduced.
   c. neglected.

7. Scientists who dig up the remains of underwater treasures
   might be called _____ archaeologists.
   a. field
   b. marine
   c. lunar

8. How would you rate the risks involved for a diver exploring the
   ocean floor?

1 2 3	4 5 6 7	8 9 10
LOW	**AVERAGE**	**HIGH**

   a. 1   b. 6   c. 9

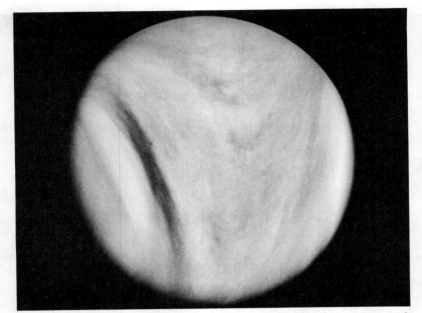

The Mystery Planet

*Which two planets in
our solar system are
thought of as twins?*

The planets Venus and Earth are roughly the same size. That is why they have been called the twins of our solar system. Venus also used to be known as the "mystery planet." Because dense, or thick, layers of clouds always cover the surface of Venus completely, astronomers were not able to see it with their telescopes.

Then, late in 1978, the *Pioneer 1* spacecraft began orbiting Venus. *Radar* (rā'där') was used to penetrate the thick layers of clouds. Radar is special equipment that uses radio waves to locate distant objects and determine what they are like. Maps were made from *Pioneer 1*'s findings.

What did these radar maps show? The largest canyon in our solar system is on Venus. The canyon is about 1500 kilometers long and about 280 kilometers wide. It is about 5 kilometers deep.

The map also indicated a ridge of mountains. The mountain ridge stands on a broad plateau that scientists think may be the result of earthquake movements. In the ridge is a volcano called Maxwell. It is about 11,100 meters high. Mount Everest, the highest mountain on Earth, is about 8700 meters high.

Scientists have identified two other mountains on Venus. These are thought to be volcanic mountains and appear to be about 7200 meters and 6300 meters high.

But the surface of Venus is very different from the surface of Earth. Scientists have learned that Venus is very hot and dry. The surface temperature on Venus is about 455°C (850°F). Slowly Venus is becoming less of a mystery.

QUESTIONS

1. Special equipment that uses radio waves to locate distant objects and determine what they are like is called _____.

2. Up until 1978, astronomers were unable to see the surface of Venus because of its thick _____ layers.

3. Compared with Mount Everest, Maxwell is
      a. broader.   b. higher.   c. deeper.

4. Some of the mountains on Venus may
      a. be volcanic.   b. have been caused by earthquakes.
      c. be lower than those on Earth.

5. Which of the following describes the surface of Venus?
      a. high and low b. smooth and flat c. gaseous and cold

Use the table to answer questions 6, 7, and 8.

SOLAR-SYSTEM STATISTICS FOR FIVE OF THE NINE PLANETS

Planet	Average Distance from Sun (in kilometers)	Diameter of Planet at Its Center (in kilometers)	Number of Years to Revolve Around Sun
Mercury	57,900,000	4,800	0.24
Venus	108,200,000	12,100	0.62
Earth	149,600,000	12,756	1.00
Mars	228,000,000	6,784	1.88
Jupiter	778,000,000	143,200	11.86

6. Compared with other planets, the planet that is farthest from the sun takes the _____ amount of time to revolve around the sun.
      a. least   b. most   c. same

7. It takes Venus _____ to revolve around the sun.
      a. more than 6 years   b. less than 1 year
      c. about 12 years

8. According to the table, the planet with the second largest diameter is
      a. Mars.   b. Jupiter.   c. Earth.

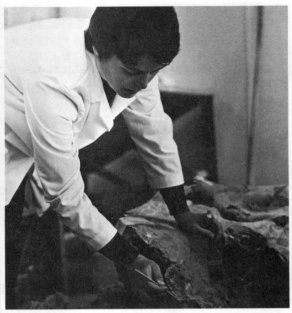

A Surprise Discovery

Animal bones were the treasures found in this gold mine.

In 1975, an important discovery was made at the bottom of an old gold mine in central Alaska. The mine is located near the mining ghost town of Jack Wade in the Yukon-Tanana uplands. However, it was not gold that was discovered in the mine, but the fossilized bones of animals nearly 30,000 years old. *Fossils* (fŏs'əlz) are the remains of ancient plant and animal life. The Jack Wade fossils were of extinct animals, that is, animals that no longer live on Earth, such as bison, musk oxen, and wooly mammoths. Lee Porter found these animal bones while earning her doctorate degree in geology.

Why was this discovery so important? In addition to dating animal activity in the area, the fossils provided *archaeologists* (är′kē ŏl′ə jĭsts) with clues to human activity. Archaeologists study the remains of past human activities. The bones had been deeply embedded in silt at the bottom of the gold mine. This means that the animals must have lived and died right near Jack Wade and were not washed ashore from somewhere else. The bones were scarred and had burn marks on them. So Porter believes that during the Ice Age in North America, early humans may have decided to use the bones as tools.

The Jack Wade fossils are one of the earliest known records of human activity in North America. The former site of the 1898 Gold Rush has turned into an archaeologists's gold mine. Lee Porter's discovery has shown how humans in search of prey, as well as shelter from advancing Ice Age glaciers, worked their way across a land bridge from Siberia to the Alaskan Yukon.

1. The word in the story that means "the remains of ancient plant and animal life" is _____ .

2. The bones that were found were from _____ animals.

3. Where were the animal bones found?

4. The animals must have lived and died near Jack Wade because the bones had been
   a. washed ashore nearby.   b. deeply embedded in silt.
   c. found right there.

5. How did Porter know that humans had also been near Jack Wade 30,000 years ago?
   a. The animal bones showed signs of human use.
   b. Humans had left behind a written record.
   c. Human bones were found with the animal bones.

6. How would you rate Porter's discovery?

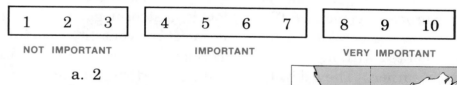

1 2 3	4 5 6 7	8 9 10
NOT IMPORTANT	IMPORTANT	VERY IMPORTANT

   a. 2
   b. 5
   c. 9

Use facts from the story and the map to answer questions 7 and 8.

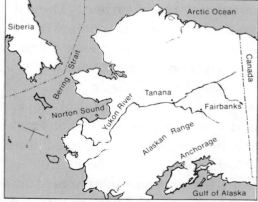

7. From which direction were early humans traveling?
   a. east to west   b. north to south   c. west to east

8. What body of water did the Siberia-to-Alaska land bridge cross?
   a. the Yukon River   b. the Bering Strait   c. Norton Sound

Eyes in the Skies

Today, most weather data is collected by machine.

During World War I, *meteorologists* (mē′tē ə rŏl′ə jĭsts), or weather scientists, did not receive reports on weather in other countries. Because of the war, communication among countries in Europe was very difficult. So a team of meteorologists in Norway experimented with new ways to predict the weather. They developed a theory that polar fronts, or masses of cold air, move down from the Arctic and affect weather around the world. Forecasting aids such as weather balloons, aerial photographs, and weather planes did not exist. So the meteorologists collected data, or information, supporting this polar-front theory from telephone and telegraph reports and fishers returning to shore. Then, this information was collected and analyzed by humans.

Today, radar, television, infrared photography, and weather satellites inform us of distant weather conditions instantly. In minutes, computers analyze and report data that it would take weeks to process by hand. For example, radar pictures provide meteorologists with data on the moisture content, structure, and location of clouds. Weather satellites orbiting Earth send back signals of the world's cloud cover. Meterologists turn the signals into pictures. They monitor, or watch, these photographs and use their knowledge of clouds to predict the weather.

Satellites monitor temperatures above Florida citrus groves. When frost is probable, growers are warned in time to heat their groves. Meteorologists are using the information collected by satellites and other modern machinery to develop new theories about the weather.

1. A polar front is a mass of _____.

2. Weather scientists are also called _____.

3. According to the story, during World War I, weather information was collected and analyzed by _____.

4. According to the story, one important way in which computers help meteorologists is by saving them _____.

5. The Norwegians contributed to the history of weather forecasting by
   a. inventing the use of infrared cameras.
   b. developing a theory of air movement.
   c. sending up the first weather satellite.

Use the chart below to answer questions 6, 7, and 8.

**MAIN TYPES OF CLOUDS AND THE
LEVELS AT WHICH THEY OCCUR**

Cloud Family	Average Height Range (in meters)	Type of Cloud	Symbol
The High Clouds	6000 to 12,000	Cirrus	Ci
		Cirrostratus	Cs
		Cirrocumulus	Cc
The Middle Clouds	1950 to 6000	Altostratus	As
		Altocumulus	Ac
The Low Clouds	480 to 1950	Stratus	St
		Nimbostratus	Ns
		Stratocumulus	Sc
The "Vertical" Clouds	480 to 12,000+	Cumulonimbus	Cb
		Cumulus	Cu

6. To which cloud family do clouds ranging in height from 1950 to 6000 meters belong?

7. Which cloud types have the greatest range in height?

8. Which symbols stand for the Low Clouds?

Getting Oil from Sand

Have you ever heard of mining oil?

A black, sticky, tar-like substance is now being mined in Alberta, a province in western Canada. This substance, called *bitumen* (bĭ tōo′ mən), is found in tar-sand deposits near the Athabasca River. It is mined in much the same way that coal is obtained from the ground—through a process known as strip mining.

The tar-sand deposits contain a heavy oil that binds the sand together. The deposits lie beneath a layer of decaying vegetation. This plant matter is scraped away by giant bucket-shaped shovels. Then, the shovels scoop up the tar-sand deposits. Next, the sticky tar sands are dumped onto conveyer belts that feed the sand into large tanks. In these tanks, hot water, steam, and air separate the bitumen from the sand. The bitumen is then chemically treated so that only a crude oil is left. To produce 1 barrel of crude oil, about 2 metric tons of the tar-sand material must be processed.

It is very costly to produce crude oil from the bitumen. However, with the rising costs of imported oil and the alarming rate at which it is being used, mined crude oil may well become an important energy source in the near future.

In the United States, Utah and California also contain deposits of tar sands. But it is believed that even more of this material is required to produce a single barrel of crude oil. So attention is still focused on the huge, rich Alberta deposits, sometimes referred to as the Saudi Arabia of tar sands.

1. The black, sticky, tar-like substance needed to make crude oil is called _____.

2. The Canadian province where tar-sand deposits are found is called _____.

3. What binds the sand together?

4. What must be removed first before miners are able to get the tar-sand deposits?
   a. decaying plants   b. chemicals   c. steam

5. After being separated from the sand, the bitumen gets
   a. dumped onto a conveyer belt.
   b. placed in huge tanks.
   c. chemically processed into crude oil.

Use the graphs below to answer questions 6, 7, and 8. The graphs show the kind of energy produced by the U. S. in 1977 and 1987.

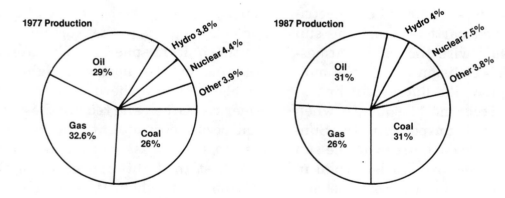

6. What was the largest kind of energy production in 1977?
   a. coal   b. gas power   c. water   d. oil

7. Which kind of enery production has grown the most since 1977? _____.

8. By how much has natural gas production changed since 1977? _____ .

Fascinating Lights: Auroras

Huge "curtains" of green and red light move slowly across the night sky. What causes these fabulous light displays?

These special, many-colored lights seen in the night skies are known as *auroras,* (ô rôr′ əz), after the Roman goddess of dawn, Aurora. We call the lights in the Northern Hemisphere the *aurora borealis* (bôr′ ē ăl′ ĭs). The lights in the Southern Hemisphere are called the *aurora australis* (ô strā′ lĭs).

Both auroras occur when electrically charged particles from the sun hit and react with the earth's atmosphere. This collision causes the molecules to glow like fluorescent lights.

Auroras occur most frequently when there is a lot of sunspot activity. Sunspots are large, dark areas on the sun where the gases are "cooler" than in the surrounding areas. Some astronomers think that sunspots are storms on the sun. These storms send tremendous streams of charged particles toward Earth.

Although auroras can occur in nearly every part of the sky, they are usually too faint to be seen except in the polar regions of the Northern and Southern Hemispheres. The aurora borealis, or the northern lights, is visible in the northern part of North America. Green and red are the colors that occur most often there, but it is also possible to see white and yellow.

At first, the lights appear low on the horizon, but when they reach full power, they may cover the entire sky. The auroras may occur in streamers and arcs of light as well as in sheets, or curtains. The constantly changing display of the auroras is one of nature's most fascinating shows.

1. The special, many-colored lights seen in the Northern Hemisphere are called _____.

2. The special, many-colored lights seen in the Southern Hemisphere are called _____.

3. The colors that occur most often in the Northern Hemisphere are _____ and _____.

4. Auroras occur only in the skies near the earth's polar regions.
        a. True   b. False   c. The story does not say.

5. Sunspots are dark because they are
       a. next to bright-colored auroras.
       b. surrounded by hotter gases.
       c. actually storms on the sun's surface.

6. After reading the story, you would conclude that people living near the equator most likely
       a. see auroras only at dawn.
       b. never see auroras.
       c. see red lights, but not white or yellow lights.

7. Fill in the missing link in the chain of events below.

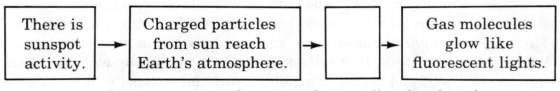

| There is sunspot activity. | → | Charged particles from sun reach Earth's atmosphere. | → | | → | Gas molecules glow like fluorescent lights. |

    a. Storms occur on the sun and give off molecules of gas.
    b. Fluorescent lights hit charged particles.
    c. Charged particles collide with gas molecules.

8. Look at the diagram below. Which letter on the diagram indicates where auroras first appear?
       a.   A
       b.   B
       c.   C

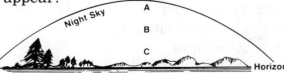

The Woman, The Dog, and The Tent

After 73 years, 3 meteorites are re-united.

Meteoroids (mē′tē ə roidz′) are stone or metal particles that revolve around the sun like very tiny planets. When part of a meteoroid falls to Earth, it is called a meteorite. The largest meteorite displayed anywhere in the world rests in the Hall of Meteorites at the American Museum of Natural History in New York City. Known as Ahnighito, or The Tent, the meteorite is composed mostly of nickel and iron and weighs over 34,000 kilograms. The name *Ahnighito* comes from an Innuit legend, or story, that tells of a woman, her dog, and a tent that fell from the sky.

The Tent and two other meteorites—The Woman and The Dog—were found in Greenland in the late 1800s. You can see Ahnighito, The Tent, in the above photograph taken at the site where the meteorites were found. In 1906, Ahnighito and the 3000-kilogram Woman were brought to the Museum of Natural History and placed near an entrance to the building. The museum's Hayden Planetarium was built around the meteorites in 1935.

Then, in 1979, both meteorites were removed from the planetarium through a huge hole that had been cut in a wall of the building. They were taken by trailer to a parking lot, where they remained under guard for 7 days. During that time, Ahnighito was hoisted into the air by a 55-meter crane. Its underside was measured, and six points were marked to show where six sturdy columns would support the meteorite in its new home.

At the end of the week, Ahnighito and The Woman were taken by truck to the museum's Hall of Meteorites. There, they were reunited with their 1-ton companion, The Dog, from which they had been separated for 73 years.

1. Stone or metal particles that revolve around the sun like very tiny planets are called _____.

2. When were the meteorites in this story found?

3. According to the story, the name *Ahnighito* comes from an _____ legend.

4. Which fact mentioned in the story gives a clue to the size of the meteorites?
   a. They were guarded for 7 days.
   b. The Hayden Planetarium was built around them.
   c. They now rest in the Hall of Meteorites.

5. After reading the story, you could conclude that
   a. meteorites can cause damage.
   b. most meteorites weigh about 3000 kilograms.
   c. meteorites are very rarely found in Greenland.

6. What was the importance of the six points on Ahnighito?
   a. They were original markings found on Ahnighito.
   b. They told the legend of the meteorites.
   c. They indicated where Ahnighito needed support.

7. People who wanted to see the meteorites in 1968 went to
   a. the Hall of Meteorites.
   b. the Hayden Planetarium.
   c. a lot near the Museum of Natural History.

8. Ahnighito would be classified as a
   a. nickel-and-iron meteoroid.
   b. stone meteorite.
   c. metal particle from space.

An Orbiting Telescope Peers into Space

How big is the universe? How old is it? How did it begin? The Space Telescope may provide some of the answers.

In the 1990s, NASA will continue to launch the space shuttle, a large vehicle that will make trips back and forth into space. On one such trip, the space shuttle will carry the Hubbel Space Telescope and place it in orbit 500 kilometers above the earth. The orbiting Space Telescope will be the largest optical instrument ever placed in space. Optical instruments help us to see objects more clearly.

The *telescope* (tĕl′ ə skōp′) uses mirrors to gather visible light, which makes observation of distant objects possible. Even objects that are too faint to be seen by the eye will be brilliantly visible in this telescope.

The telescope will be used to study space objects such as stars, galaxies, planets, and comets. Light from these objects will enter the open end of the telescope and will then be projected by a large mirror onto a smaller mirror.

From there, the light will be directed toward scientific instruments in the back of the telescope. These instruments will take pictures and measure the distance of space objects as well as determine their makeup. The information will be beamed back to astronomers at Earth stations.

Why is it necessary to have the Space Telescope? One reason is that clouds and bad weather can prevent accurate viewing of space objects from telescopes on Earth. In space, there is an absence of weather as we know it on Earth. So the Space Telescope will be able to provide astronomers with a clear view of the universe.

1. A telescope gathers _____ light and makes it possible to observe distant objects.

2. The Space Telescope will orbit the earth at a height of _____ kilometers.

3. To gather visible light, a telescope uses _____.

4. Poor viewing of space objects from telescopes on Earth is caused by
    a. clouds.   b. sunlight.   c. darkness.

5. After light passes onto the smaller mirror of the Space Telescope, it
    a. gets projected onto a larger mirror.
    b. is directed toward instruments in the back of the telescope.
    c. passes out the open end of the telescope.

6. Which of the following is *not* a function of the scientific instruments?
    a. to measure the distance of space objects
    b. to photograph Earth from space
    c. to discover what space objects are made of

7. Which of the following would *not* be an optical instrument?
    a. a microscope   b. a pair of glasses   c. a television

8. How would you rate the ability of the Space Telescope to view the universe?

1 2 3	4 5 6 7	8 9 10
POOR	**GOOD**	**EXCELLENT**

    a. 3   b. 6   c. 10

The Weather Can Affect Your Life

Can weather affect the way you feel and act?

There is a growing belief among behavioral scientists that, indeed, weather does have an effect on our daily lives. According to Dr. Stephen Rosen, an expert on weather and human behavior, there are many ways in which weather affects us. As Dr. Rosen explains it, weather is a form of stress, and its changes will result in stressful effects on the body.

Although our bodies adapt to changes in the weather, we are not always prepared for sudden weather changes and extremes in temperature. For example, in warm weather, blood vessels *dilate* (dī lāt'), or expand, to allow the body to get rid of excess heat. In cold weather, the blood vessels constrict, or tighten, keeping warmth in the body. Either change in the blood vessels triggers other bodily changes, for example, in body chemistry, blood composition, and the amount of oxygen going to the brain. It is this last change that most directly affects our mood and behavior. With a sudden change in the weather, we may feel happy and full of energy one day, depressed and run-down the next.

Extremes in temperature also affect people who take medication. For example, when you take aspirin, it causes the blood vessels to dilate, which in turn causes the body to lose heat more quickly. Other types of drugs or medication will affect the body differently according to the type of weather.

So it is important for people to be aware of the effects of weather and take medication under a doctor's supervision. Keeping in touch with your body's needs may mean tuning in to tonight's weather forecast.

1. In the story, the word _____ means "to expand."

2. Dr. Rosen describes weather as a form of _____.

3. What happens to a person's blood vessels in cold weather?

4. Unless you are under a doctor's orders, you probably should not take too many aspirins in _____ weather.
       a. hot   b. damp   c. cold

5. Which of the following statements *best* expresses the main idea of the story?
       a. Weather forecasts can predict your health.
       b. Changes in the weather affect people's lives.
       c. Medication should never be taken in excess.

Use the table below to answer questions 6, 7, and 8.

TIPS FOR WARM AND COLD CLIMATES

	Warm or Hot Weather	Cold Weather
Eat	salads, vegetables, and carbohydrates such as breads and cereals.	meats, cheese, milk, eggs, and other foods high in protein and fat.
Drink	lots of water and other fluids; replace water hour by hour.	normal amounts of liquid.
Avoid	emotional stress, long periods of heavy work outdoors.	too much dry heat, long periods of heavy work outdoors.

6. During hot weather, your body _____ liquids.
       a. retains   b. loses   c. stores

7. In cold climates, you are advised to eat foods rich in _____ and _____.

8. What should you avoid in *both* hot and cold weather?

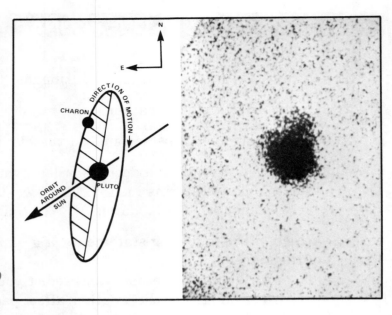

Pluto and Charon: Two Celestial Bodies

Pluto and its moon were discovered in much the same way.

On June 22, 1978, James W. Christy was working at the U.S. Naval Observatory examining some photographic plates of the planet Pluto. He looked at the photographs that had been taken by telescope in Flagstaff, Arizona. Christy soon realized that he had discovered a new *celestial* (sə lĕs′ chəl) body, a moon of Pluto! The word *celestial* is used to describe something related to the sky or the heavens. This new moon was given the identification number 1978-P-1. Christy suggested the name *Charon* (kâr′ ən).

Charon is estimated to be about 1250 kilometers in diameter and takes about 6.4 days to revolve around, or circle, Pluto. As it orbits, Charon stays close to Pluto, only about 15,300 kilometers away. In the photo of Pluto (above, left), Charon looks like a flare at the top of the planet and a little to the right.

Pluto was discovered in much the same way. Dr. Percival Lowell believed there was another planet in the universe. He had worked out a mathematical formula indicating the planet's supposed location. Many photographs of this celestial area were taken with a telescope. Then, in 1930, 14 years after Lowell's death, Clyde W. Tombaugh was working in Flagstaff. Looking through photographic plates, he discovered an object, a new celestial body. Tombaugh had sighted the outermost planet in the solar system, Pluto.

Some astronomers think that once Pluto may have been a moon of the planet Neptune and that it was knocked out of orbit during an interplanetary "accident".

1. The word used to describe something related to the sky or the heavens is _____.

2. How was Pluto's moon first identified?
   a. by name   b. by number   c. by location

3. According to the story, some scientists believe that at one time Pluto may have been a moon of _____.

4. Which scientist was responsible for estimating where Pluto was located in space?

5. The discoveries of Pluto and Charon were similar in that both bodies
   a. were discovered by the same person.   b. had been photographed by telescope.   c. were sighted in the same year.

6. Pluto is about 2600 kilometers in diameter. According to information in the story, Charon's diameter would be
   a. less than half that of Pluto.   b. twice that of Pluto.
   c. about the same as Pluto's.

Use the table to answer questions 7 and 8.

The Planets in Order of Distance from the Sun	Period of Revolution Around the Sun
Mercury (the closest)	88 days
Venus	225 days
Earth	365 days
Mars	687 days
Jupiter	12 years
Saturn	$29\frac{1}{2}$ years
Uranus	84 years
Neptune	164 years
Pluto (the farthest)	247 years

7. The planet that takes the longest time to revolve around the sun is the
   a. farthest away from the sun.   b. fourth planet from the sun.
   c. closest planet to the sun.

8. Compared with Earth, it takes Uranus _____ more years to revolve around the sun.

Clean Water Makes a Difference

Polluted water—people cannot drink it. Fish cannot live in it. Plants cannot "breathe" in it.

In the late 1960s, the life in rivers, lakes, and tidewater areas was dying. Chemicals, raw sewage, and pesticides were dumped into the water. Both visible and invisible pollutants filled the rivers, and there was serious concern that pollution would eventually ruin many bodies of water all over the world.

Pollution is especially damaging to a body of water called an *estuary* (ĕs′ chōō ĕr′ē). An estuary is a bay at the mouth of a major river where salt water and fresh water mix. Estuaries are rich in nutrients and support the growth of great amounts of *phytoplankton* (fī′ tō plăngk′ tən). Phytoplankton—tiny, floating plants—serve as a source of food for young fish. Many large cities, such as New York, Boston, San Francisco, and London (England), are located on estuaries. Household and industrial wastes from cities are sometimes dumped into the estuaries. Small amounts of waste fertilize the bays, but large amounts can actually poison the water life.

Today, the results of laws to eliminate or cut down on pollution can be seen in many places. For half a century, the Connecticut River and its tributaries were filled with pollutants. But since 1975, salmon, which are especially sensitive to pollution, have been caught in the river. Lake Erie, once thought of as beyond rescue, is also showing signs of life. A rugged fish called the alewife has returned to the waters of Lake Erie. Perhaps, in time, the world's waters will be rescued after all.

1. A body of water at the mouth of a major river where salt water and fresh water mix is called an _____.

2. In the story, the tiny, floating plants that are a source of food for young fish are called _____.

3. Three forms of pollution mentioned in the story are chemicals, raw sewage, and
   a. fertilizers.   b. pesticides.   c. nutrients.

4. According to the story, we know that the pollution in the Connecticut River is beginning to clear up because
   a. some salmon have been caught in the river.
   b. there is more plant growth in the river.
   c. the water looks much cleaner.

5. Dumping very small amounts of waste into an estuary
   a. helps encourage the growth of phytoplankton.
   b. poisons the water forever.
   c. kills the source of food for young fish.

6. One sure sign that the pollution in a body of water is decreasing is when
   a. you can no longer see any pollutants in the water.
   b. plants cannot float on the water.
   c. the plant and animal life return to the water.

7. You could conclude from the story that water pollution is
   a. a minor problem.
   b. an international problem.
   c. no longer a problem.

8. Fill in the missing link in the chain of events below.

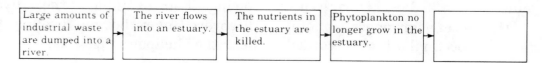

| Large amounts of industrial waste are dumped into a river. | The river flows into an estuary. | The nutrients in the estuary are killed. | Phytoplankton no longer grow in the estuary. | |

Jacques Piccard, Deep-Sea Explorer

One of the best-known oceanographers in the world is Dr. Jacques Piccard. He is a scientist who studies and explores the ocean depths.

In 1969, Dr. Piccard and a group of oceanographers took an amazing underwater voyage aboard a 15-meter submarine called the *Ben Franklin*. The oceanographers wanted to learn more about the Gulf Stream, a current of water about 80 kilometers wide and 600 meters deep. The Gulf Stream flows along the Atlantic Coast of the United States.

The *Ben Franklin* drifted 2400 kilometers up the Gulf Stream from the east coast of Florida to Nova Scotia. The journey took 30 days. During this time, the oceanographers photographed the ocean bottom, recorded the temperature of the water, and observed the current.

Exploring the ocean depths is not new to Piccard. His father and he were among the first to plan and build bathyscaphes, the round-shaped vessels used to explore the ocean depths. Bathyscaphes must be built to withstand the pressure of the water at great depths.

In 1960, Jacques Piccard and Donald Walsh set the world's record for deep diving. The picture above shows Piccard (on the right) with Walsh aboard the bathyscaphe *Trieste*. The 2 men dove 10,800 meters to the floor of the Mariana Trench in the Pacific Ocean. This dive paved the way for other explorers of deep-sea marine life. Following their example, other divers discovered more bottom-dwelling life near the Galapagos Islands.

A Visit to the Los Angeles County Natural History Museum

As you know, fossils are the remains of plants and animals that lived long ago. Geologists study fossils to learn what life on Earth was like thousands, and even millions, of years ago.

Many museums in North America have fossil collections. One such museum is the Natural History Museum in Los Angeles, California. Visitors can see large fossil collections of birds; mammals; fish; turtles; insects; spiders; and, of course, dinosaurs.

One of the dinosaurs is the *Tyrannosaurus rex,* a meat-eating dinosaur that lived more than 65 million years ago. Scientists estimate that the tyrannosaurus was about 6 meters tall and 15 meters long and weighed about 6 metric tons.

If visitors are interested in watching scientists at work, they can go to the

George C. Page Museum, a branch of the Natural History Museum.

In the Page Museum, visitors can observe scientists digging carefully for fossils in large, open pits. Over the years, scientists have uncovered more than 1 million fossils in these pits. The fossils include the remains of animals such as vultures, camels, bears, wolves, and saber-toothed tigers, which are now extinct. These animals were trapped in the pits hundreds of thousands of years ago.

A Prehistoric Walk

The hikers are taking a path that leads right into the age of dinosaurs. Find the brontosaurus, the pteranodon (flying dinosaur), and the ferocious *Tyrannosaurus rex*.

A Solar-System Crossword

Can you solve the crossword puzzle? If you need help, use the word list below.

Across

1. the planet closest to the sun
5. the planet you live on
6. the circular path in which an object revolves around another object
7. a body that travels around the sun and has a head and a tail
10. a bright star
12. the sixth planet of the solar system
13. a star that suddenly becomes brighter than normal
14. the highest part of the sky, directly overhead

Down

1. the fourth planet of the solar system
2. a satellite of the earth
3. sometimes called a shooting star or a falling star
4. a person who trains to travel in a spacecraft
8. a large collection of stars and gases and dust that is found in outer space
9. the fifth planet of the solar system
10. any one of the nine bodies that orbit the sun
11. the star that supplies the energy which sustains life on Earth

Word List

galaxy   meteor   sun   Earth   comet   astronaut   planet   moon   nova
zenith   orbit   Mercury   Saturn   Jupiter   Polaris   Mars

SCIENCE ADVENTURES

Investigating the World Around You:

Environmental Problems

Neighborhood overcrowding, noise, air pollution, and water pollution. These are some environmental problems seen in many communities. People cause many of these problems.

Walk around your home or school for about an hour. Identify as many environmental problems as you can. Make a list of the problems you see. Also, note the possible cause for each. Use a chart similar to the one below. Compare your list with those of your classmates. Think of different ways to solve some of these problems.

ENVIRONMENTAL PROBLEMS AND HUMAN BEHAVIOR

Problem	Possible Cause

How can you keep your local environment from becoming worse? How can you improve your local environment?

Finding Out About Street Covers

Beneath the streets of your neighborhood are many pipes and cables. Openings are placed in streets so people can reach these.

Take a walk around your neighborhood. List all the different kinds of covers you can find. Describe each one. Include size, color, and the material it is made of. Note whatever writing may be found on it. You should easily find telephone-company covers (T + Co.). Look for Traffic-Department plates (fire alarm, street light, traffic signal). Watch for Water Department covers (water meter), storm-drain covers, and other covers.

What do you think is underneath the covers you found? Where do the pipes or wires come from? Where do they go?

Do Not Remove or Tamper with Any Cover You Find.

Call or visit your electric company and gas company. Visit your Water Department or another agency. These organizations can provide information about what is underneath the covers.

Comparing Building Materials

Find out about the materials used to build a city.

What are curbs made of?

What are streets made of?

What are sidewalks made of?

Compare a sidewalk with a street. How are they similar? How are they different?

What is a curb made of? How is this material similar to sidewalk material? How is it similar to street material?

How is curb material different from street and sidewalk material?

Write your observations on a chart similar to the one below.

BUILDING MATERIALS

Location	Material	Characteristics
Sidewalk		
Curb		
Street		

Producing Some Environmental Art

Science creates both dangerous and helpful conditions in your community. You could take pictures of these things with a camera. Then you could make a design using these pictures.

Take a walk around your home or school. Collect materials for making a collage, a painting, a sculpture, or a mobile.

Try to show an environmental problem with your work.

Your art might show how science improves the environment.

PHYSICAL SCIENCE

Helicopters seem to ignore gravity. Lifted into the air by large spinning propellers, helicopters can do many things other aircraft cannot do. They can fly straight up or straight down. They can fly sideways, backward, and forward, and they can even hover or turn around in one spot. A helicopter can use almost any cleared space for takeoff and landing. This aircraft is especially valuable for rescue operations, aerial observation, and transportation in areas that have no roads or airfields.

Biking with Science on Your Side

Be a champ! Win the race against friction.

The riders bend low over their bicycles and grip their handlebars. The signal is given for the 2-kilometer race to begin. Soon, the riders are whizzing along the track—first at 30 kilometers per hour, then at 50. They reach speeds of up to 65 kilometers per hour. Finally, speeding across the finish line at 82 kilometers per hour, comes the winner, Number Nine!

There is only one prize winner in a bike race, but all the riders win the race against *friction* (frĭk′shən). Friction is a problem that all moving objects have to overcome. It is a dragging force that opposes, or resists, the movement of one surface against another.

Friction is what makes sandpaper work. If you rub a piece of wood across a piece of sandpaper, some of the wood comes off. Friction is the force that wears away some of the wood. But if you rub the wood against a smooth piece of paper, no wood is worn away. The friction is less when two smooth surfaces move against each other. The amount of friction will also decrease when one or both objects are wet, or lubricated. Weight is also an important factor in the race against friction. The lighter the bike rider is, the less friction there is and the greater the speed.

A bike rider has to overcome air friction, or air resistance. When a bicycle racer bends over the handlebars, rider and bicycle make a smooth, low shape that can move faster through the air. Thin, hard bicycle tires also help reduce friction as the tires move over the track.

Of course, *some* friction is needed to get started and to brake, or stop. But the less friction, the more speed. And here comes Number Nine now!

1. Friction is a dragging _____ that opposes the movement of one surface against another.

2. A bicycle rider has to overcome _____ resistance.

3. The heavier a bike's rider is, the greater the amount of _____.

4. Which of the following would probably cause the *most* friction?
   a. rubbing two rough surfaces against each other
   b. rubbing a smooth surface against a rough one
   c. rubbing two smooth surfaces against each other

5. If a bike rider bends low over the handlebars, the amount of air friction she or he experiences
   a. increases.   b. decreases.   c. remains the same.

Use the table to answer questions 6, 7, and 8.

BRAKING DISTANCES

Distance a Car Will Travel after Driver Applies Brakes		
Car Speed (in kilometers—km)	Wet Surface (in meters)	Dry Surface (in meters)
16	2.4	1.8
32	9.6	7.2
48	21.6	16.2
64	38.4	28.8
80	60.0	45.0
96	86.4	64.8
112	117.6	88.2

6. The greater the car speed, the _____ the car comes to a complete stop on either surface.
   a. more slowly   b. faster   c. more easily

7. Before coming to a complete stop, a car will travel _____ distance on a wet surface as compared with a dry surface.
   a. the same   b. a greater   c. a shorter

8. On a dry surface, at which speed below could a driver bring a car to a complete stop most quickly?
   a. 96 km per hour   b. 64 km per hour   c. 32 km per hour

Hidden Homes, Buried Buildings

Today, architects are building down under instead of up above.

Rock caves and dirt-bank cellars are examples of *subterranean* (sŭb′tə rā′ nē ən), or below-ground-level, structures. They may sound like cold, uncomfortable places, but both caves and subsoil maintain almost constant temperatures. In New England, the air temperature meters below the ground is 10°C, regardless of the temperature of the air above ground. The air temperature at the entrance to a cave can be 35°C, but a hundred or so meters inside, the air temperature is a steady 11°C, summer or winter. In Kansas City, Missouri, over 100 companies employing 2,000 people have subterranean offices in limestone caverns.

"Earth-sheltered" structures are also being built. Unlike the subterranean type, earth-sheltered structures are not truly underground. They might be built into a hillside or halfway below ground level. For example, an elementary school in Virginia was built into a hillside, and only its solar

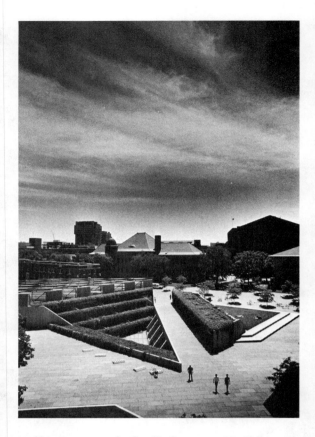

collectors and skylight are visible. It costs half as much to heat and cool this school as it does similar schools in the same area.

"Aren't earth-sheltered homes damp and cold and slimy and dark?" people ask. No, they don't have to be. Skylights and windows, set into the slope of the earth, let in light and sunshine.

There are some drawbacks to building down, however. The condition of the soil must be right. Hard rock or moist, swampy areas would not be good building locations. Also, it is fairly difficult and costly to add on to subterranean and earth-sheltered structures.

1. In the story, the word that refers to structures built below ground level is _____ .

2. The air temperature in caves and subsoil _____ as the air temperature outside rises.
       a. rises slightly   b. remains steady   c. falls sharply

3. Living in a cave is a dark and gloomy existence.
       a. True   b. False   c. The story does not say.

4. Which of the following is *not* true of earth-sheltered buildings?
       a. They are cheaper to heat and cool.
       b. They maintain constant year-round temperatures.
       c. They can be built anywhere.

5. During which season would the air temperature of New England subsoil be most useful to people living in earth-sheltered homes?
       a. summer   b. fall   c. winter

Use the table to answer questions 6, 7, and 8.

EARTH-SHELTERED AND SUBTERRANEAN BUILDINGS

Place	Terrain or Setting	Type of Structure	Natural Temperature
Waxahachine, Texas	3 meters below ground level	House	15 to 17°C
Reston, Virginia	Built into a hillside	Elementary school	Not available
University of Minnesota Williamson Hall	Below campus level	Bookstore	Never below 10°C
Kansas City, Missouri	Limestone caverns 15 to 60 meters deep	Industrial park	14°C

6. What type of structure was built in limestone caverns?

7. In this table, the warmest natural temperature below ground level occurs in _____ .

8. Which structure listed in the table would be called earth-sheltered?
       a. the school   b. the industrial park   c. the bookstore

A Solar Balloon

Floating high above the city, he could hear only the sounds of his own cheers.

Frederick Eshoo spent more than 2 years designing and testing his *aerostat* (âr' ō stăt'), the technical word for a hot-air balloon. Eshoo's aerostat, which he named *Sunstat,* uses the sun as its energy source. All aerostats rise when the air inside them is heated. This happens because the heated air inside the balloon is lighter than the cooler air outside.

How does *Sunstat* use the sun's energy? One side of *Sunstat* is transparent, allowing the sun's light rays to pass through it. The other side is made of black material. Because the transparent side is curved, it acts like a lens, focusing the sunlight onto the inner surface of the balloon. The black inner surface collects, or absorbs, the sun's heat. Then, as air circulates inside the balloon, it is heated on the black side and distributed, or spread, throughout the balloon. The uppermost part of the black collector is actually a curtain that can be opened or closed to control the amount of light entering the aerostat.

Eshoo placed small battery-operated propellers on either side of the aerostat to rotate the balloon from one side to the other. *Sunstat* rises when its transparent side is turned toward the sun and descends when the outer surface of its black side faces the sun. This happens because the outer surface is a shiny layer that reflects light instead of absorbing it. *Sunstat*'s design and engineering may provide the key to future solar-powered aircraft and space vehicles.

QUESTIONS

1. In the story, the technical word for a hot-air balloon is _____.

2. The source of energy for Eshoo's hot-air balloon is _____.

3. The curved, transparent side of the balloon acts like a _____.

4. The purpose of the propellers is to control the balloon's
       a. height.   b. speed.   c. air distribution.

5. *Sunstat* works on the principle that
       a. hot air is heavier than cold air.   b. heated air rises.
       c. cool air is lighter than warm air.

6. If Eshoo wanted to descend in his balloon, he would
       a. steer the transparent side so it faces the sun.
       b. open up the curtain on the heated side.
       c. turn the shiny outer surface toward the sun.

7. When sunlight is reflected off the balloon's shiny surface, the air inside
       a. cools off.   b. rises.   c. heats up.

Use the drawing to answer question 8.

Sunstat
(Altitude = 1 kilometer)

Mount Alta
(Height = $1\frac{1}{2}$ kilometers)

8. You are the *Sunstat's* pilot. What must you do to go over the mountains?
       a. rotate the balloon so its transparent side faces the sun
       b. use the battery-operated propellers to increase the balloon's air speed
       c. rotate the balloon so its shiny surface faces the sun

Fuels of the Future

Gasohol and liquid hydrogen may be the fuels of the future.

Gasohol is a fuel produced by mixing about 10 percent alcohol with 90 percent gasoline, which is a product of oil. The mixture is used to power automobiles. Unlike the oil used to produce gasoline, alcohol is a renewable resource made from plants. Possible sources of alcohol are sugar, wheat, potatoes, and corn. Scientists are also testing ways to make alcohol from industrial wastes.

By using gasohol, the United States can reduce the amount of oil it imports from other countries. Experts estimate that we may save as much as 200 million barrels of oil each year. Gasohol has another advantage over gasoline. Because gasohol burns cleaner than gasoline, it produces fewer pollutants. Also, in engines that are designed to use it, gasohol is about as efficient as gasoline.

A second new fuel source is hydrogen. Unlike oil, hydrogen is plentiful. Also, very little pollution is created when hydrogen burns. In fact, when hydrogen mixes with oxygen during burning, ordinary water is

formed. All water contains some hydrogen, so hydrogen can be obtained from many different sources, even seawater.

One way to separate hydrogen from water is by *electrolysis* (ĭ lĕk trŏl′ĭ sĭs). Electrolysis is a process in which a current of electricity is passed through water, causing the water molecules to split into hydrogen and oxygen. The hydrogen can then be collected, changed into liquid form, and transported easily and cheaply by pipeline or tanker. Pipelines could bring hydrogen directly to homes and factories for heating purposes and to "gas" stations for use in automobiles.

QUESTIONS

Use the list of words below to complete questions 1 through 4.
gasohol   fuel   electrolysis   alcohol

1. A current of electricity is passed through water, separating it into hydrogen and oxygen. This process is called _____.

2. In the story, a mixture that burns cleaner than gasoline is _____.

3. Something that is burned to produce energy is called a _____.

4. In the story, a renewable resource made from plants is _____.

5. How will the use of gasohol affect oil imports to the United States?
    a. Oil imports will increase.
    b. Oil imports will decrease.
    c. Oil imports will remain the same.

6. According to the story, when compared with gasoline, gasohol
    a. is about as efficient.
    b. costs much more.
    c. produces pollutants.

7. The hydrogen fuel discussed in the story would come under the heading of
    a. Liquids.   b. Solids.   c. Gases.

8. Hydrogen gas is lighter than gasoline, but it takes up a lot of space. In what way would this be a problem with today's cars?
    a. The cars' engines would need to be heavier.
    b. The cars' fuel tanks would have to be enlarged.
    c. The cars would need larger pollution-control devices.

Does Your Car Have a Brain?

A little wonder called the microprocessor is the "brain" behind the computer car.

The *microprocessor* (mī′krō prŏs′ĕs′ər) is a very small computer. It is a small, etched chip made of a chemical element called *silicon* (sĭl′ĭ kən). Chips are made in batches of thousands on wafer-thin sheets of silicon. Thousands of transistors and other electronic parts are etched onto these chips.

This is how the microprocessor will work in a car. Located in a container behind the car's engine, the microprocessor will be connected to three sensors. The sensors will monitor, or watch, the engine's cooling and exhaust systems as well as the flow of fuel. Information from the sensors will be fed into the microprocessor, where it will be analyzed. If any part of these systems is not operating properly, that information will be flashed onto a display screen mounted on the car's instrument panel.

The microprocessor is already being used for another purpose in some automobiles. The trip computer shows the driver information such as the car's current kilometers per gallon, the speed, the engine temperature, the estimated time of arrival, and the number of kilometers to go before the end of the trip. It even displays how many kilometers the car can go before running out of fuel.

Perhaps the most interesting use of the microprocessor in the future will be for an alertness test. The driver who does not pass this test will not be able to start the engine. The "brain" in the computer car is truly a little wonder.

1. The microprocessor is a very small _____

2. The microprocessor is made of the chemical element _____.

3. Thousands of electronic parts are etched onto
       a. chips.   b. wafers.   c. boxes.

4. After information about the car's engine is analyzed, it may be
       a. monitored for correctness.
       b. fed into the microprocessor.
       c. flashed onto a display screen.

5. According to the story, the trip computer will *not* show the driver
       a. the best route to the destination.
       b. the number of kilometers per gallon of fuel.
       c. the approximate time of arrival.

6. This story would lead you to conclude that microprocessors are
       a. already in use in some cars.
       b. not yet in operation.
       c. a good idea, but not very useful.

7. Which of the following uses of the microprocessor is *most* likely to reduce accidents?
       a. the engine-control system
       b. the alertness test
       c. the trip computer

8. How would you rate the microprocessor's effect on the automobile industry?

1 2 3	4 5 6 7	8 9 10
NOT GREAT	**GREAT**	**VERY GREAT**

    a. 2   b. 6   c. 10

Solar Energy Can Get You into Hot Water!

Want to get into hot water? Use a solar water heater.

The sun provides the earth with an enormous amount of energy. Two weeks' worth of solar energy would equal the combined energy in all the earth's known supply of fossil fuels—coal, oil, and natural gas. Solar energy itself is free, but costly equipment is needed to collect and convert, or change, sunlight into usable energy.

An essential and costly part of a solar-energy system is the solar collector. The most common type of solar collector is the flat-plate collector, which works well in areas where the temperature is moderate. One promising use of this collecting-and-converting equipment is for heating water.

To heat water, solar collectors are placed on the roof of a building. The sun's light rays pass through the collectors' covers, which can be made of glass, fiberglass, or certain types of plastic. The heat from the sun's rays is absorbed by the flat collection plate underneath. The plate is usually black or dark in color to absorb as much of the sun's heat as possible. Water circulates through pipes, or tubing, attached to this black surface. The absorbed heat warms the water. Heated water, ready for use, then flows through the pipes into the building.

The various parts of the solar-energy system are held in a container made of metal, fiberglass, or wood. The container is insulated with certain kinds of foam or fiberglass to lessen heat loss.

In Israel, almost one out of every five homes has a solar water heater. This is so partly because Israel has a sunny climate. Also, Israel must import all of its heating fuels. Japan has a similar fuel problem and is currently using more than 2 million solar water heaters.

1. In the story, the word *convert* means the same as _____.

2. Coal, oil and natural gas are all examples of _____.

3. Solar energy works on the principle of changing _____ into usable energy.

4. According to the story, solar energy is a good value for Israel and Japan, because both countries
    a. must import all of their heating fuels.
    b. use very little fuel anyway.
    c. can make cheaper solar collectors.

5. A solar-energy system *must* depend on _____ in order to work.
    a. moderate temperatures
    b. the sun's heat
    c. hot water

Use the diagram below to answer questions 6, 7, and 8.

CROSS SECTION OF A FLAT-PLATE COLLECTOR

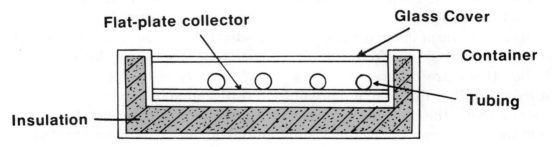

6. Water flows through the _____, which is attached to the _____.

7. Before the sun's rays strike the flat-plate collector, they must pass through the _____.

8. The part of the collection system that lessens heat loss is located inside a metal, fiberglass, or wood _____.

A Wonderful Tool: The Laser

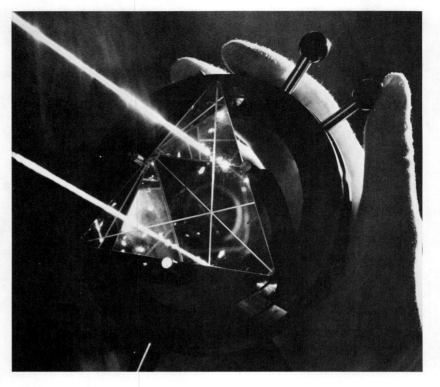

Lasers are no longer science fiction.

A doctor has discovered a detached *retina* (rĕt′n ə) in a patient's eye. In the past, a detached, or torn, retina might have meant a loss of sight in the eye. But today, an amazing tool makes delicate eye surgery easier. The tool is a *laser* (lā′ zər), a powerful beam of light. In certain cases, by carefully directing this light beam, the doctor can mend the retina.

Basically, the laser beam is the same kind of light that shines from a lamp bulb, but there are differences. The light from a bulb is diffused, or spread out, over a room; the light from a laser travels in a very narrow beam. The energy of the laser light is extremely intense and is focused in one direction.

Physicists have found that by shining light through certain crystals or gases, they can keep the light from spreading. The laser light becomes *amplified* (ăm′plə fīd′), or stronger, as two mirrors reflect it back and forth many times. Finally, it passes through a hole in the center of one mirror as a burst of very intense light. The word *laser* stands for "Light Amplification by Stimulated Emission of Radiation." You can see why it is easier simply to say "laser."

A variety of lasers are available to do different jobs. In industry, a laser's light energy can become heat to weld, or mend, metal parts and to burn away dirt from stone buildings. Lasers are also used in hospitals. The heating action of laser light beams can sterilize instruments or weld tiny blood vessels during delicate surgery. In communications, a laser beam can carry many voice messages and television signals at the same time.

1. In the story, when something is amplified, it is made
   _____ .

2. Pieces of metal can be welded together by using the _____
   produced by laser light beams.
       a. gas   b. heat   c. crystals

3. In this story, the doctor is going to use a laser beam to
       a. sterilize instruments before an operation.
       b. keep a patient from losing too much blood.
       c. save a patient's eyesight.

4. One major difference between lamplight and laser light is that
   lamplight
       a. is much brighter than a laser.
       b. spreads out in all directions.
       c. contains more heat than a laser.

5. Together, the mirrors in this story act like
       a. a flashlight.
       b. a surgeon's needle.
       c. an amplifier.

6. How is laser light made stronger?
       a. by passing it through a small hole
       b. by reflecting it back and forth many times
       c. by shining it through certain crystals or gases

Use the diagrams below to answer questions 7 and 8.

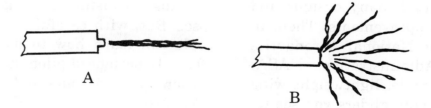

A   B

7. Which diagram shows light energy in a very diffused form?

8. In which diagram would light energy be stronger?

Gliding Through Air

A colorful object floats over a hill-side. Is it a bird? Is it a plane? No! It's a hang glider!

Recently, the sport of hang gliding has been growing in popularity. But the idea of building a glider that floats on air is actually very old. (A glider is a light, engineless aircraft with wide wings designed for long periods of soaring, or gliding.) For hundreds of years, people tried to find ways to fly like birds. Leonardo da Vinci designed a glider model in the fifteenth century. Over the years, many people died trying to fly gliders that were too large, too heavy, and too hard to handle.

Inventors tried many designs and made many improvements. Then, in the 1960s, the National Aeronautics and Space Administration (NASA) perfected a simple, lightweight wing design. The hang gliders you see today use NASA's design.

Hang gliders are now smaller and much easier to control than earlier models. The pilot hangs underneath the wings in a harness and holds on to a trapeze-like bar to steer the glider. If the pilot moves forward, the nose drops and the glider picks up speed. If the pilot moves backward, the nose rises and the glider loses speed. The pilot moves from side to side to turn the glider.

It sounds easy, but hang gliding can be very dangerous. Pilots must learn how to control their gliders in sudden updrafts of air. Sometimes hang gliders climb too steeply and the wings stall, or stop flying. A stall can lead to a crash. A crash may also occur if the glider makes too sharp a downward angle, causing the wings to collapse. But, with careful instruction, people can learn how to hang glide safely. Experienced pilots have traveled for up to 15 hours and as far as 48 kilometers.

1. According to the story, a glider is a light, _____ aircraft with wide _____ designed for long periods of gliding.

2. The idea of human flight
   a. is not very popular.
   b. has been around for hundreds of years.
   c. was proved to be impossible.

3. Why didn't early gliders work?
   a. The wings were much too small.
   b. They were hard to control.
   c. They were too light.

4. What part of the glider supports the pilot?
   a. the wings   b. the harness   c. the nose

5. When hang gliding, what could be the result of either a sharp downward angle or a very steep climb?

Complete the following chart to answer questions 6, 7, and 8.

HANG GLIDING

Action Performed by Pilot	Result of Action
Moves forward	Nose drops, glider _____ speed 6
Moves backward	Nose rises, glider _____ speed 7
_____ 8	Glider turns

Trash: Something of Value

There is treasure to be found in garbage dumps all across the country.

What treasure could be in rotting potato peels and moldy chicken bones? The treasure is called methane. Methane is an odorless, colorless gas that can be burned to obtain energy. This energy can be used to make electricity to light and heat buildings.

A garbage dump is a perfect factory for methane. The *organic* (ôr găn' ĭk) waste materials found in garbage dumps serve as food for tiny bacteria. Organic matter comes from living things such as plants or animals. As the bacteria digest the organic garbage, they make methane. Over the years, as one load of garbage is piled on top of another, the amount of methane increases. Methane is a flammable gas, or one that is easily set on fire. In fact, some garbage dumps are so full of methane that they sometimes catch fire.

People in New Jersey found out about the treasure in their garbage dumps when they decided to turn one such refuse site into a large park. They knew they would have to get rid of the dangerous methane beneath the garbage. A gas company offered to buy the methane for its customers.

To get the methane out, the gas company will drive long pipes deep into the garbage dump. Then, the gas will be pumped out into other pipes leading to people's homes. What some people sent out of their homes as garbage will go back into other people's homes as energy.

1. Matter that comes from living things such as plants or animals is called _____ matter.

2. In order for people to obtain energy from it, methane must be _____.

3. The energy obtained from methane can be used to make _____ to heat and light buildings.

4. The methane in a garbage dump _____ as the amount of garbage piles up.
       a. increases   b. decreases   c. remains the same

5. It would be difficult to tell that a pipeline containing methane was leaking, because methane is _____ and _____.

6. Fill in the missing link in the chain of events below.

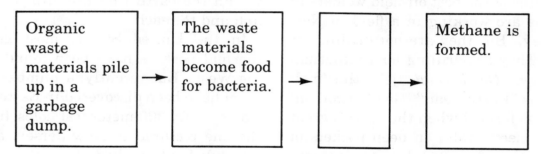

Organic waste materials pile up in a garbage dump.	→	The waste materials become food for bacteria.	→		→	Methane is formed.

7. Which of the following would you be most likely to see on a sign at the entrance to a garbage dump?
       a. Quiet Zone
       b. No Smoking
       c. Littering Prohibited

8. Methane would be classified as a kind of
       a. organic waste.
       b. gas.
       c. bacterium.

Drilling for Hot Water

Why are these Texas oil-field welders drilling for hot water?

Three of the best oil-field welders in Texas are working in a field in New Jersey. But they are not drilling for oil. They are drilling for geothermal energy. *Geothermal* (jē'ō thûr'məl) means "Earth heat." Geothermal energy is formed when the earth's great heat meets water in deep pockets of rock. Heat from 32 kilometers or more below the earth's surface seeps up slowly into the rock pockets. When water seeps down and meets this heat, it also becomes very hot.

This extremely hot water shoots upward with great force. Where there are cracks in the earth's surface, the water forces its way through in the form of *geysers* (gī'zərz). "Old Faithful," in Yellowstone National Park, is a geyser that releases geothermal energy in the form of steam and hot water. But most geothermal energy still lies trapped in rock pockets deep within the earth that are difficult to find and to reach.

In the United States, most geothermal pockets have been found in the West. But recently, a number of them have been discovered in Eastern states. Fifty 300-meter test holes, like the one pictured in New Jersey, are scheduled to be drilled. If geothermal energy is found along the East Coast, it will be different from that now used in the West, where it is used mainly to generate electricity. Because of lower temperatures in these Eastern areas, the geothermal energy will be too cool to generate electricity. Instead, it will be used to heat and cool homes and office buildings. Scientists will continue to study the possible uses of geothermal energy in the East. Will it be worthwhile?

1. The word *geothermal* means _____.

2. Geothermal energy is formed when the earth's great heat meets
   a. water.   b. steam.   c. rock.

3. Where is geothermal energy formed?
   a. in valleys just below the earth's surface
   b. in shooting geysers above the earth
   c. in rock pockets deep within the earth

4. Geothermal energy in the West is _____ than geothermal energy in the East.
   a. cooler   b. hotter   c. wetter

5. What forms when there are cracks in the earth's surface?

6. Which of the following is *not* true of geothermal energy?
   a. It is mostly available in the West.
   b. It is easy to reach.
   c. It is used to generate electricity.

Use the diagram below to answer questions 7 and 8.

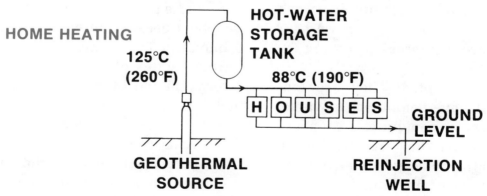

HOME HEATING

HOT-WATER STORAGE TANK

125°C (260°F)

88°C (190°F)

H O U S E S

GROUND LEVEL

GEOTHERMAL SOURCE

REINJECTION WELL

7. How hot (°C) is the water as it flows to the storage tank?

8. After being used to heat homes, any excess, or extra, water probably goes
   a. into the atmosphere.   b. back into the earth.
   c. into the storage tank.

Is There a Robot in Your Future?

Wanted: New employees for dangerous factory work. Only robots need apply.

Robots may soon be the answer to the problem of how to fill many working positions in our factories. Robots have certain advantages over human beings. Because they do not get tired, robots can produce work at a much steadier rate than humans can. Robots can produce high-quality work day after day, and they can work at jobs that are dangerous or boring for human beings.

What are robots? They are machines that have flexible, or movable, *appendages* (ə pĕn′dĭj ĕz′). Appendages are parts that are attached to a main body. Some robots have arm-like appendages, making it possible for them to perform human tasks. Unlike most machines, a robot can be "taught," or programmed, to do a number of jobs in different ways.

There are already more than 5,000 robots at work in routine jobs throughout the world. Auto manufacturing is one industry that is finding these mechanical helpers useful. A single robot in a car plant can take the place of two human workers. The robot lifts heavy parts into place on autos as they move down the assembly line. Plants that handle radioactive materials also use robots, because the work is a threat to human safety. By the end of the century, some plants will be completely manned by robots on the assembly line.

Will robots ever be able to take over for humans completely? Not really. After all, robots are nothing more than machines. Some scientists are working on artificial intelligence for robots. Through the use of computer programs, some robots will have decision-making abilities. But it will be up to people to program and supervise these activities.

1. In this story, the word that refers to parts attached to a main body is _____.

2. In the story, the word *program* means the same as
    a. produce.   b. instruct.   c. ask.

Decide whether the descriptions below refer to robots, humans, or both. Write the letter R if the statement refers to robots, H if it refers to humans, and B if it refers to both.

3. ____ They get bored with their jobs now and then.

4. ____ They never get tired from too much work.

5. ____ They can do more than one kind of job.

6. A factory owner might want to use robots instead of humans for some jobs, because in the long run robots _____ humans.
    a. are smarter than
    b. cost less than
    c. will take the place of

7. An automobile factory uses robots to move heavy car parts from one place to another. One of the robots puts an entire set of parts in the wrong place. Who is responsible for this mistake?
    a. the robot   b. the programmer   c. no one

8. An advertisement in the "Help Wanted" section of a newspaper states that the job demands a great deal of extra work, or overtime, and requires a lot of decision making. The manager would most likely hire

    a. a human.   b. a robot.   c. either a human or a robot.

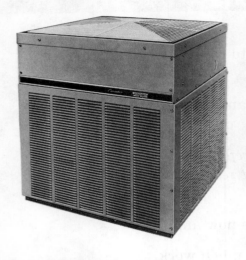

Moving Heat Around

A heat pump can be used to heat and cool buildings.

Imagine a machine that can *absorb* (ăb sôrb'), or soak up, heat and then pump the heat where it is needed. There is such a machine, and it is called a heat pump. Heating engineers think that the heat pump could be used to heat large buildings. This would mean that increasingly expensive fuels, such as gas and oil, could be put to other uses. A heat pump would be less expensive to use and could save energy, too.

The heat pump absorbs most of its heat from outdoors, even in winter. Everything, whether hot or cold, contains some heat. Cold things just have less heat than warm things. During winter, a heat pump absorbs heat from the air outdoors and transfers it inside to heat the air indoors. The heat pump must work *against* the principle that

heat will always move from warm things to cold things. You can actually see this principle at work on a hot day. Look at the hood of a car that has been driven a long distance. The wavy lines you see over the hood are waves of heat leaving the hot car engine and moving into the cooler air.

The heat pump works by reversing this natural flow of heat. It can do this because it is filled with a special liquid that absorbs heat. As it flows through tubes, the liquid absorbs heat from the outdoor air. Then, the heated liquid boils and changes into a vapor, or gas. Next, the vapor is superheated and pumped through indoor tubes. Now that the vapor is hotter than room temperature, it condenses, or turns back into a liquid. The heat pump removes the heat from the liquid and pumps it into the building's heating pipes.

1. A heat pump is a machine that can soak up, or _____, heat from indoors or outdoors.

2. A heat pump gets most of its heat from _____.

3. According to the story, one important advantage of using a heat pump is that it can help save _____.

4. Unlike most other heating systems that use energy to *create* heat, a heat pump uses energy to _____ heat that is already available.
    a. save
    b. transfer
    c. store

5. What would happen if you changed a building's heat pump so that it worked in the opposite way?
    a. The building would get cooler.
    b. Nothing would happen.
    c. It would get colder outside.

6. In a glass of ice water, is the heat moving from the ice to the water or from the water to the ice? The heat moves from the _____ to the _____.

7. Which of the following would be an example of how heat flows naturally?
    a. snow melting   b. a fan turning   c. water boiling

8. A heat pump may be *twice* as efficient as a regular heating system when the temperature outdoors is 10°C, but only slightly more efficient when the temperature is 2°C. So areas where the winter temperature range is _____ would make the *most* efficient use of a heat pump.
    a. −10 to −2°C
    b. −2 to 2°C
    c. 2 to 7°C

A Steady and Welcome Wind

Citizens in Denmark joined together to cut energy costs.

For years Denmark was known as a land of windmills. But, by the 1930s, most of them were no longer used because it seemed old-fashioned. Yet the winds from the North Sea continued to blow across Denmark's flat Jutland peninsula at a high *velocity* (və lŏs′ĭ tē), or speed.

Today, this steady north wind is welcome. With a velocity of over 6 kilometers per hour, it makes wind-generated electricity practical. Scientists estimate that the wind blows about 300 days a year. And since there are few forests and no mountains in Denmark to break the wind, it is a powerful wind, indeed.

On the western edge of Jutland, a giant windmill is now at work. The windmill was built by citizens in the area who wanted to prove to the world how wind can be converted, or changed, into energy cheaply. The windmill stands 80 meters high in Ulfborg, Jutland. Sitting atop a 54-meter-high tower are 3 giant fiberglass propellers, each 27 meters long. The tower is made of concrete and steel at the top. The fiberglass blades can bend, but will not break, in strong winds that can reach hurricane strength.

Electrical power is measured in a unit called the *kilowatt* (kĭl′ə wŏt′).

A kilowatt-hour is the use of 1 kilowatt of power for 1 hour. The Jutland windmill can produce 4 million kilowatt-hours of electrical power in 1 year. That is enough to provide electricity for 2,800 people. There are also several smaller windmills around the country. At Windmill Park near the city of Ebeltoft, a cluster, or group, of windmills provides electricity for many nearby families.

1. In the story, the word that means "speed" is _____.

2. Electrical power is measured in a unit called the _____.

3. Denmark's wind comes from the _____.

4. According to the story, Denmark is a good place to use wind power because there are
   a. many windmills left over from the 1930s.
   b. no mountains and few forests to slow down the wind.
   c. fewer people to provide with electrical power.

5. What makes fiberglass a good material for the propeller blades on a windmill?
   a. It is flexible but strong.   b. It is inexpensive to use.
   c. It allows light to pass through.

6. Under which of the following headings would you list the Jutland windmill?
   a. Citizens' Efforts   b. Free Electrical Power
   c. An Unsteady Tower

Use the table to answer questions 7 and 8.

AVERAGE WIND SPEEDS AT SOME WEATHER STATIONS IN THE UNITED STATES (computed through 1977)

Location	Average Speed (in kilometers per hour)	Location	Average Speed (in kilometers per hour)
Bismarck, N.Dak.	16.8	Detroit, Mich.	16.3
Boston, Mass.	20.2	Galveston, Tex.	17.6
Buffalo, N.Y.	19.7	Key West, Fla.	17.9
Cape Hatteras, N.C.	18.6	Minneapolis, Minn.	16.8
Chicago, Ill.	16.6	Omaha, Nebr.	18.9
Cleveland, Ohio	17.3	San Francisco, Calif.	16.8

7. In which location would a wind-powered generator be least efficient?

8. In which two cities is the velocity of the wind the greatest?

127

Constant Energy from the Sun

As electric bills increase and fossil fuels decrease, free and plentiful sunlight looks brighter and brighter.

Radiation from the sun can be converted, or changed, directly into electricity in several ways. But, at the moment, the most promising way makes use of a device called the *photovoltaic* (fō′tō vŏl tā′ĭk), or solar, cell. Developed in the early 1950s, photovoltaic cells have been widely used aboard space vehicles and as battery chargers aboard boats. Simply stated, the conversion of solar radiation into electrical energy takes place when sunlight hits certain materials in the photovoltaic cell and forms an electric current.

In the 1980s, NASA launched a space shuttle. The shuttle is just the beginning of regular cargo service back and forth into space. One of the shuttle's jobs will be to put into orbit a permanent Satellite Solar Power Station. The power satellite will be kept in a fixed orbit about 36,000 kilometers above a giant receiving antenna on Earth.

The satellite's 2 wing-like solar panels, each about 5 kilometers wide, will contain thousands of 2-centimeter by 2-centimeter photovoltaic cells. To increase their power, the cells will be connected electrically to each other. The sun's light rays will strike the cells and be converted to electrical energy. Then, the electrical energy will be beamed to Earth in the form of microwaves, picked up by the giant Earth-based antenna, and reconverted to electrical energy. In space, the sun shines 24 hours a day, there are no clouds, and solar radiation is much greater than on Earth. The amount of solar energy received by a power satellite would be as much as 15 times greater than that received by an Earth-based panel.

The big 25-meter antenna in the photograph above is being used by NASA as a research tool. Engineers are studying the problems involved in using solar-power satellite stations.

1. Another name for *photovoltaic cell* is _____.

2. The purpose of the photovoltaic cell is to convert solar radiation to _____.

3. Connecting photovoltaic cells to each other electrically will _____ their power.

4. All solar-energy systems are dependent upon
   a. the sun.   b. electrical energy.   c. photovoltaic cells.

5. Compared with Earth-based panels, the solar panels on a power satellite will
   a. receive constant sunlight.
   b. not be dependable as sources of energy.
   c. be able to produce electrical energy without photovoltaic cells.

6. Why will it be necessary to keep the power satellite in a fixed orbit above Earth?
   a. to make sure that microwaves from the satellite can be beamed to a particular receiver
   b. to make sure the solar panels receive sunlight directly during the day
   c. to increase the power of the Earth-based antenna

7. If many Satellite Solar Power Stations could be put into orbit around Earth, then it is possible that
   a. electrical energy would become increasingly expensive.
   b. our dependence on energy would decrease.
   c. we would no longer need to depend on fossil fuels.

8. Fill in the missing link in the chain of events below.

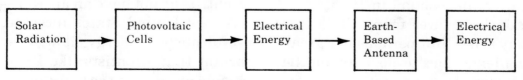

a. Sunlight   b. Microwaves   c. Solar Panels

129

Dr. Shirley Jackson

When Shirley Jackson was born in Washington, D.C., no one could have foreseen that she would become one of the first Black women to enter the field of atomic research.

Upon completion of her elementary and secondary education, Shirley enrolled at the Massachusetts Institute of Technology. When she finished her undergraduate studies at M.I.T., she received numerous awards and scholarship offers from schools such as Harvard University and Brown University. However, she decided to complete graduate school at M.I.T. and went on to earn her Ph.D. in physics. After graduation, Dr. Jackson went to work for Fermi National Accelerator Laboratory. The Fermi Laboratory was named after Enrico Fermi, the Italian physicist who developed the first self-sustaining nuclear chain reaction in 1945.

Dr. Jackson faces many challenges as a physicist. But perhaps her greatest challenge has to do with matter and energy. *Matter* is defined as anything that has weight and takes up

space. All matter is made up of tiny particles called atoms. At the center of an atom is its nucleus. Inside the nucleus are protons, which have a positive electrical charge, and neutrons, which have no electrical charge. What force holds the protons and neutrons of a nucleus together? Scientists do not have an answer—yet.

As the United States increases its use of nuclear energy, it will be important that scientists like Dr. Jackson find answers to the many questions related to the atom.

A Visit to the Fernbank Science Center

Any time of the year is a good time to visit the Fernbank Science Center in Atlanta, Georgia. Every year, more than 700,000 people from the United States and other countries visit the center.

The Fernbank Science Center is surrounded by a large forest that has several walking trails. Visitors use special guide sheets that contain interesting facts about the plants and animals that live in the forest. Some of the trees along the trails are marked for identification, and one of the trails was built especially for blind visitors.

The center also has one of the largest planetariums in North America. The planetarium can project over 8,000 stars that are visible in the night skies.

In the Fernbank Exhibit Hall, visitors can see things such as rock and mineral collections, telescopes, petrified wood, meteorites, and some of the Georgia animals that live in Fernbank Forest.

The center provides many kinds of programs for students and adults, and these programs go on all year long. For example, there are classes on how to use a computer, how to grow a vegetable garden, how to make a bird feeder, and how to use an electron microscope. The center is certainly an interesting and rewarding place to visit.

An Aeronautics Crisscross

How well will you fly with this puzzle? The following words have to do with aeronautics, the science of aircraft production and operation. Fill in the spaces with the words listed below.

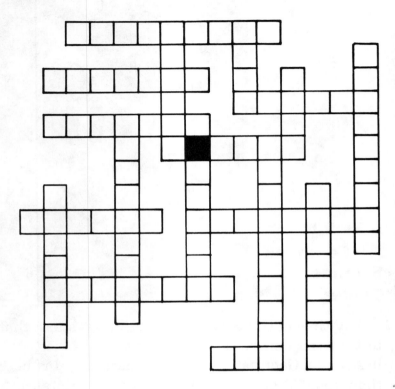

3-Letter Word

fin

4-Letter Words

drag
lift
wing

6-Letter Words

glider
rocket
beacon
thrust

7-Letter Words

airship
propjet
compass

8-Letter Words

fuselage
ailerons
altitude

9-Letter Words

altimeter
propeller
dirigible

10-Letter Word

navigation

Do You Know Your Elements?

In chemistry, a substance that cannot be broken down by chemical means is an element. Aluminum is an element. See if you can find the names of 19 other elements in the hidden-word game. The words go across, down, and diagonally. If you need help, use the Word List below.

```
S I L V E R C Z I N C
U R R O T X H T H M O
L O L O I E L U C A P
F E B I N E O N A N P
U L A O H A R G O N E
R A R D Y T I S O O R
H E L I U M N T B L A
Y D I N G Y E E O E D
D M X E N O N N R D O
C A R B O N C H O R N
O N I T R O G E N I C
```

Word List

GOLD IODINE IRON LEAD HELIUM BORON XENON
CHLORINE COPPER CARBON NITROGEN NEON SILVER
ARGON SULFUR TIN TUNGSTEN ZINC RADON

Making an Electric Quiz Board

To make an electric quiz board, you will need:

1. a sheet of pegboard or cardboard
2. paper fasteners
3. insulated electrical wire
4. a battery
5. a bulb and bulb holder
6. question–answer cards to put on the finished quiz board

Decide how many question–answer cards you want to put on the front. Fifteen of each would be good. But you might decide on some other number. The cards can be cut to size. The size will depend on the cardboard or pegboard you are using.

Make wire connections as shown on the next page. The connections should be changed from time to time. This way, others won't find out how your board is wired.

Some suggestions for question–answer topics follow:

1. chemical elements–symbols
2. star patterns–constellations
3. countries–capitals
4. states–capitals
5. sporting events–player or team names
6. dates–events

Front view of a quiz board

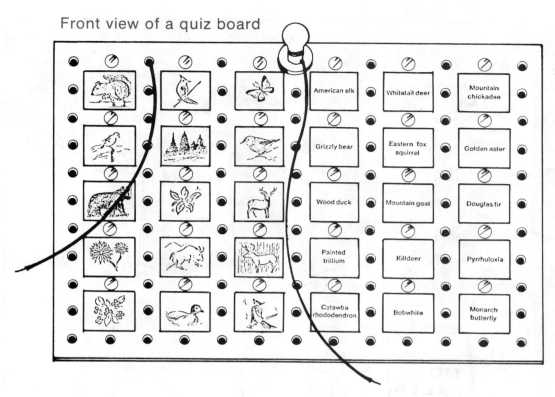

			American elk	Whitetail deer	Mountain chickadee
			Grizzly bear	Eastern fox squirrel	Golden aster
			Wood duck	Mountain goat	Douglas fir
			Painted trillium	Killdeer	Pyrrhuloxia
			Catawba rhododendron	Bobwhite	Monarch butterfly

Back view of a quiz board with the first two wires attached

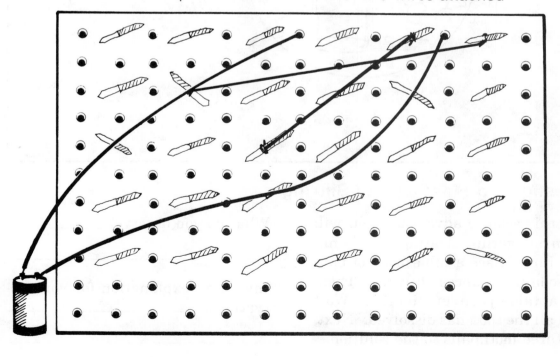

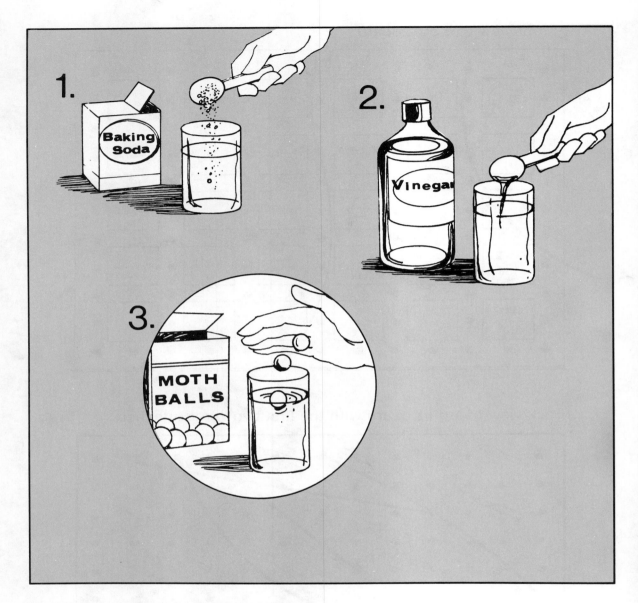

Investigating Floating and Sinking

In this science adventure, you will be investigating floating and sinking. First, place a tablespoon of baking soda in 6 ounces of water. Then, add a tablespoon of vinegar. Wait until all the soda has dissolved. Next, add three mothballs to the solution.

What do you observe? _____

_____

Invent an explanation for your observations: _____

_____

Do the following activities. (Note: You might have to change your explanation because of what you find out.)

Check an encyclopedia or some other reference book.

What is Archimedes' Principle?

_____

_____

_____

Conduct an experiment to see if Archimedes' Principle is true. This picture should give you some good hints.

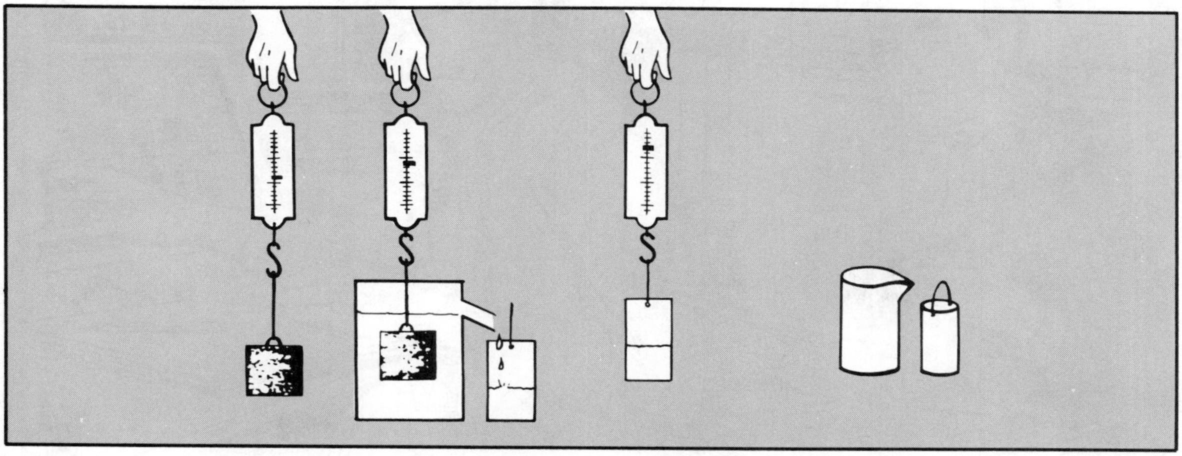

Describe your experiment: _____

_____

_____

_____

_____

Give a revised explanation of the mothball behavior:

_____

_____

_____

_____

_____

CAREERS IN SCIENCE

"Well, here we are."

"Yeah. High school. They're telling us that we have to prepare for life."

"Big deal. I'm having trouble with life right now!"

"My counselor says I have to take math."

"They tell everybody that."

"And science, too."

"Yeah. They tell everybody that, too."

"The counselor told me that math and science were important for my life."

"Oh? Are you going to do experiments every day of your life?"

"I don't think so. But we're supposed to learn how a lot of things work, and we will do some experiments to learn how scientists go about doing stuff. Mrs. Katz called it the scientific method. That's supposed to help us learn to think."

"Yeah, right—you're going to learn a method to make a million bucks."

"Oh, come on."

"So why don't they just show us a movie?"

"It's like everything else. You learn best if you do it yourself.

You can't learn to dance, play basketball, or type by watching a movie."

"So I'm an expert in cutting up dead frogs or in making door bells ring. How am I ever going to use that? And what about the other stuff you have to learn in math and science? I mean, who's ever going to use it?"

"You are. I am. We all are."

"How?"

"What if you want to go into a science-related career?"

"Why would I want to do that? Besides, scientists just sit around in white laboratories in little white coats and run funny experiments with animals and coils and stuff."

"Not quite."

"There are all sorts of careers in science and science-related fields. Why, you told me yourself that you were interested in computers. Now, that's a science career. You need both math and science for that."

"Yeah, I guess so. Hey—I've got a career that you don't need science for. I'd like to be a professional basketball player."

"Professional sports? How about the coaches and the trainers? They had to have science to learn about the human body. And coaching itself is a kind of science. Take the statistics of a game. Let's say you are hitting 0.678 from the floor. That takes math to figure. And what about the people who design the equipment? They had to take science to learn how to do that."

"Okay, okay. But I still don't see why I have to cut up dead animals."

"Why, to learn how your own body works. You see, the frog is an animal, even if it isn't exactly like you."

"Come to think of it, maybe it is like you."

"Huh?"

"Well, you are always jumping around, and you like to swim. And just now, you have the same green color that a frog does, and . . . "

"What did I do to deserve this?"

So what are you interested in? Check around. Do some research. Find out what science-related careers there are in your area of interest. What sort of work do people in those careers do?

How much money do they make?

What kind of schooling do you have to have to work in those careers?

Are there a lot of opportunities in those fields?

For additional information, look in the *Career Opportunities Handbook* put out by the U.S. Department of Commerce.

Answer the following questionnaire. Then discuss your answers with a teacher, your parents, or your guidance counselor. This is one way to discover what kind of career would suit you best.

1. What kind of things are you interested in?
2. What are some science-related careers in your area of interest?
3. Which of these science-related careers interest you most? Why?
4. Which of these science-related careers interest you least? Why?
5. Which of the following career-related factors do you consider most important?
   a. Work will be close to home.
   b. There will be some travel.
   c. You will be traveling all the time.

6. What do you think is your most important career motivation?
   a. money
   b. fame
   c. self-satisfaction
   d. a need to do useful work

7. What are the educational requirements for your chosen career?
   a. high school
   b. 2-year college degree
   c. 4-year college degree
   d. graduate school
   e. trade school
   f. technical school

8. Does your career require a good knowledge of
   a. mathematics?
   b. physical science?
   c. life science?
   d. Earth science?
   e. other ____ ?

9. Does your school offer the kinds of courses that would prepare you for advanced study in your career choice?
   a. Yes   b. No

10. Read the following statement:
    "There is a conflict between the needs of a technological society and the necessity for maintaining ecological balance."
    Do you
    a. agree with the statement?
    b. disagree with the statement?

11. IF YOU AGREE: What can you do, if you choose the science-related career in this questionnaire, to resolve the conflict between technology and ecological balance?

12. IF YOU DISAGREE: What conditions would have to exist to cause such a conflict to arise? What can you do, if you choose the science-related career in this questionnaire, to prevent this conflict from occurring?

A city of
the future?

Life in the future may be very different from life today. In your chosen science-related career, how would you be affected by any of the topics listed below? Choose one topic for a report. Discuss as many of the others as you can with your friends.

How would you be affected . . .

1. if people's bodies could be frozen in suspended animation and brought back to life later?
2. if people worked 4 hours a week?
3. if all food were replaced by a single pill?
4. if everybody were assigned a number and an occupation at birth?
5. if all transportation were by antigravity belt?
6. if cloning were a simple, normal procedure?
7. if self-sufficient cities were built under the oceans?
8. if we made contact with intelligent life from outer space?
9. if a way were discovered to stop aging?
10. if time travel became a normal vacation?

What changes would you like to see in society and technology?
What would you want to do, within your chosen science-related career, to make those changes?

WORDS TO KNOW

The following words are found in the stories throughout this book. The words are listed according to the page on which they appear.

Many of the science books and magazines that you use contain some or all of these words. So it is important that you know the meaning of each word as it is used in science. This will make it easier for you to read and understand science materials.

Use a dictionary or a glossary of science terms to find the meanings and pronunciations of those words that are not familiar to you. You may want to record this information in your own personal "word bank."

LIFE SCIENCE UNIT

p. 14
actually
algae
although
common
continue
examined
inspect
microscopes
probably
shafts
solution
source
species
sufficient
theory

p. 16
available
breed
caribou
control
coyotes
elk
endangered

example
extent
extinct
extinction
increase
link
mammals
population
predators
preserve
reduced
result
species

p. 18
active
considered
digests
extinct
extremely
horny
lowlands
monitor lizard
reptiles
saw-like
slender
species
therefore
tremendous

type
usually

p. 20
abdomen
common
familiar
injects
poisonous
prey
probably
produce
ranging
recluse
special
species
strand
tarantulas
thorax
usually
victims

p. 22
biologist
circulate
currents
development
environment
incubator

lingcod
marine
organisms
predators
promote
protective
restock
rudder
survival
themselves

p. 24
according
depths
edible
grown
legend
numerous
predator
prey
pursuing
unique
unusual

p. 26
alcohol
bushy
cattails
graceful
merely

methane
pellets
process
rhizomes
source
tend

p. 28
breeding
extinct
fetch
immediately
mate
preyed
throughout
wardens

p. 30
according
bacteria
biologists
depths
exploratory
hemoglobin
layers
minerals
nourishing
oxygen
plastic
protective
sifts
submersible
unlike
unusual

p. 32
calories
carbohydrates
concerned
constantly
develop
dietitians
information
minerals
niacin
nourish
nutrients

nutritious
oxygen
proteins
tacos
varying

p. 34
characteristic
complex
complicated
developed
distinct
dolphins
echolocation
emit
employ
fascinated
fishnets
frequency
information
intelligent
mammals
missions
rescue
systems
vocal

p. 36
beeline
behavioral
clustering
dense
efficient
landmark
nectar
organized
pollinate
process
sources
syrup

p. 38
according
anosmia
granted
information
molecules

movement
phantom
phantosmia
senses
sensitive
theory
usually

p. 40
beneficial
considered
molt
nymphs
predator
preys
range
role
survive

p. 42
arteries
cholesterol
circulatory
  system
common
content
ensure
establishing
hypertension
reduce
regularly
sensibly
serious
stress
substance
veins

p. 44
abdomen
chelipeds
depths
hermit
locomotion
plastic
protective
thorax

unlike
withdraws

p. 46
common
develop
fungi
fungus
identify
mass
mycelium
spores
strands
unlike
usually

p. 48
activity
anemones
barnacles
creature
extends
litters
mussels
pier
pilings
pillars
pry
sift
sponges
themselves
urchins

p. 50
analyzed
determines
efficient
electronic
  device
guarantee
information
laboratory
oxygen
role
tackler

particles
reunited
revolve
sturdy
trailer

p. 84
absence
accurate
astronomers
brilliantly
comets
determine
galaxies
information
observation
optical
projected
telescope

p. 86
according
adapt
aware
composition
constrict
depressed
dilate
effects
excess
extremes
latter
medication
mood
oxygen
stress
supervision
tighten

p. 88
astronomers
celestial
Charon
diameter
estimated
mathematical

outermost
realized
related
revolve
solar system

p. 90
actually
alewife
concern
eliminate
especially
estuary
eventually
household
industrial
located
nutrients
pesticides
phytoplankton
pollutants
pollution
rescue
sensitive
serious
sewage
source
tidewater
tributaries

PHYSICAL SCIENCE UNIT

p. 102
factor
friction
lubricated
movement
opposes
overcome

resistance
resists

p. 104
architects
caverns
condition
constant
drawbacks
limestone
maintain
regardless
skylight
slimy
solar
structures
subsoil
subterranean
uncomfortable

p. 106
absorbs
actually
aerostat
aircraft
circulates
descends
designing
distributed
focusing
layer
operated
solar
source
technical
throughout
transparent
uppermost

p. 108
advantage
alcohol
created
current
efficient
electrolysis
estimate

gasohol
hydrogen
molecule
obtained
oxygen
pipeline
pollutants
process
produces
purposes
resource
sources
transported
unlike
wastes

p. 110
analyzed
electronic
etched
exhaust
information
microprocessor
monitor
operating
sensors
silicon
systems
transistors
wafer-thin

p. 112
absorbed
common
convert
currently
essential
fiberglass
fossil fuel
insulated
lessen
moderate
plastic
plate
solar

KEEPING A RECORD OF YOUR PROGRESS

The Progress Charts on these pages are for use with the questions that follow the stories in the Life Science, Earth-Space Science, and Physical Science Units. Keeping a record of your progress will help you to see how well you are doing and where you need to improve. Use the charts in the following way:

After you have checked your answers, look at the first column, headed "Questions Page." Read down the column until you find the row with the page number of the questions you have completed. Put an X through the number of each question in the row that you answered correctly. Add the number of correct answers, and write your total score in the last column in that row.

After you have done the questions for several stories, check to see which questions you answered correctly. Which ones were incorrect? Is there a pattern? For example, you may find that you have answered most of the literal comprehension questions correctly but that you are having difficulty answering the applied comprehension questions. If so, then this is an area in which you need help.

When you have completed all the stories in a unit, write the total number of correct answers at the bottom of each column.

PROGRESS CHART FOR LIFE SCIENCE UNIT

Questions Page	Science Vocabulary	Comprehension Question Numbers			Total Number Correct per Story
		Literal	Interpretive	Applied	
15	1	2,3	4,5,6,7	8	
17	1,2	3	4,5,6	7,8	
19	1	2,3	4,5	6,7,8	
21	1	2,3,4	5,6	7,8	
23	1	2,3	4,5,6	7,8	
25	1	2,3	4,5,6,7	8	
27	1	2,3,4	5,6,7	8	
29	1	2,3	4,5,6,7	8	
31	1	2,3	4,5	6,7,8	
33	1	2	3,4	5,6,7,8	
35	1	2,3	4,5	6,7,8	
37	1	2,3	4,5	6,7,8	
39	1,2	3,4	5,6,7	8	
41	1	2,3	4,5,6	7,8	
43	1,2,3	4	5,6	7,8	
45	1	2,3,4	5,6	7,8	
47	1	2,3,4	5	6,7,8	
49	1	2,3,4	5,6,7	8	
51	1	2	3,4	5,6,7,8	
53	1,2	3	4,5,6	7,8	
Total Correct per Question Type					

PROGRESS CHART FOR PHYSICAL SCIENCE UNIT

Questions Page	Comprehension Question Numbers				Total Number Correct per Story
	Science Vocabulary	Literal	Interpretive	Applied	
103	1	2,3	4,5	6,7,8	
105	1	2	3,4,5	6,7,8	
107	1	2,3	4,5,6,7	8	
109	1,2,3,4		5,6	7,8	
111	1	2,3	4,5,6,7	8	
113	1	2,3	4,5	6,7,8	
115	1	2,3,4	5,6	7,8	
117	1	2,3,4	5	6,7,8	
119	1	2,3,4	5	6,7,8	
121	1	2,3	4,5,6	7,8	
123	1,2	3,4,5	6	7,8	
125	1	2,3,4	5,6	7,8	
127	1	2,3,4	5,6	7,8	
129	1	2,3	4,5,6,7	8	

Total Correct per Question Type

PROGRESS CHART FOR EARTH-SPACE SCIENCE UNIT

Questions Page	Comprehension Question Numbers				Total Number Correct per Story
	Science Vocabulary	Literal	Interpretive	Applied	
65	1,2,3	4	5	6,7,8	
67	1	2,3,4	5	6,7,8	
69	1	2,3	4,5	6,7,8	
71	1	2,3,4	5,6,7	8	
73	1	2,3,4	5	6,7,8	
75	1	2,3,4	5	6,7,8	
77	1,2	3	4,5	6,7,8	
79	1	2,3	4,5	6,7,8	
81	1,2	3,4	5,6	7,8	
83	1	2,3	4,5,6,7	8	
85	1	2,3,4	5,6	7,8	
87	1	2,3	4,5	6,7,8	
89	1	2,3,4	5	6,7,8	
91	1,2	3	4,5,6,7	8	

Total Correct per Question Type

BIBLIOGRAPHY

Books on Life Science

Amon, Aline. *Roadrunners and Other Cuckoos*. New York: Atheneum, 1978.

Ault, Phil. *These Are the Great Lakes*. New York: Dodd, Mead, 1972.

Batten, Mary. *The Tropical Forest: Ants, Animals, and Plants*. New York: Crowell, 1973.

Bright, Michael. *Pollution & Wildlife*, Survival Series. New York: Gloucester Press, 1987.

Cochrane, Jennifer. *Land Energy*, Project Ecology Series. New York: Bookwright Press, 1987.

Cooper, Gale. *Inside Animals*. Boston: Atlantic: Little, Brown, 1978.

Epstein, Sam and Beryl. *Dr. Beaumont and the Man with the Hole in His Stomach*. illustrated by Joseph Scrofani. New York: Coward, 1978.

Gilbert, Sara. *Feeling Good: A Book About You and Your Body*. New York: Four Winds Press, 1979.

Hess, Lilo. *Secrets in the Meadow*. New York: Scribners, 1980.

Hutchins, Ross E. *Nature Invented It First*. New York: Dodd, Mead, 1980.

Laycock, George. *Death Valley*. New York: Four Winds Press, 1976.

Leen, Nina. *Snakes*. New York: Four Winds Press, 1976.

Limburg, Peter. *What's in the Name of Wild Animals*. illustrated by Murray Tinkleman. New York: Coward, 1977.

McLaughlin, Molly. *Earthworms, Dirt, & Rotten Leaves: An Exploration in Ecology*. New York: Atheneum, 1986.

Malatesta, Anne and Ronald Friedland. *The White Kikuyu: Louis S. B. Leakey*. New York: McGraw-Hill, 1978.

Patent, Dorothy Hinshaw. *Animal and Plant Mimicry*. New York: Holiday, 1978.

Pringle, Laurence. *City and Suburbs: Exploring an Ecosystem*. New York: Macmillan, 1975.

_____. *Listen to the Crows*. New York: Crowell, 1976.

Selsam, Millicent E. and Joyce Hunt. *A First Look at Owls, Eagles, & Other Hunters of the Sky*, A First Look At . . . Series. New York: Walker, 1986.

Wise, William. *Animal Rescue*. illustrated by Heidi Palmer. New York: Putnam's Sons, 1978.

Books on Earth-Space Science

Angrist, Stanley W. *Other Worlds, Other Beings*. New York: Crowell, 1973.

Branley, Franklyn M. *Black Holes, White Dwarfs, and Superstars*, Exploring Our Universe Series, illustrated by Helmut K. Wimmer. New York: Crowell, 1973.

Gallant, Roy A. *Beyond Earth: The Search for Extraterrestrial Life*. New York: Four Winds Press, 1977.

_____. *Earth's Changing Climate*. New York: Four Winds Press, 1979.

_____. *Fires in the Sky: The Birth and Death of Stars*. New York: Four Winds Press, 1979.

Laycock, George. *Beyond the Arctic Circle*. New York: Four Winds Press, 1978.

_____. *Caves*, illustrated by DeVere E. Burt. New York: Four Winds Press, 1976.

Mercer, Charles. *Monsters in the Earth*. New York: G. P. Putnam's Sons, 1978.

Pollard, Michael. *Air, Water, Weather*. New York, Facts on File, 1987.

Simon, Barbara B. *Volcanoes; Mountains of Fire*. Chicago: Childrens Press, 1976.

Sterling, Philip. *Sea and Earth: The Life of Rachel Carson*. New York: Crowell, 1974.

Taylor, L. B., Jr. *Gifts from Space: How Space Technology is Improving Life on Earth*. New York: Crowell, 1977.

Vogt, Gregory. *An Album of Modern Spaceships*, Picture Album Series, New York, Watts, 1987.

Books on Physical Science

Berger, Melvin. *Atoms, Molecules, & Quarks*. New York: Putnam, 1986.

Chase, Sarah B. *Moving to Win: The Physics of Sports*. New York: Messner, 1977.

Chester, Michael. *Particles: An Introduction to Particle Physics*. New York: Macmillan, 1978.

Books on Physical Science

Cross, Wilbur. *Solar Energy*, Science & Technology Series. Chicago: Childrens Press, 1984.

Dennis, Landt. *Catch the Wind: A Book of Windmills and Windpower*. New York: Four Winds Press, 1976.

Gallant, Roy A. *Fires In the Sky—The Birth and Death of Stars*. New York: Four Winds Press, 1979.

Halacy, Dan. *Nuclear Energy*. New York: Watts, 1984.

Lewis, Bruce. *Meet the Computer*. illustrated by Leonard Kessler. New York: Dodd, Mead, 1977.

Schneider, Herman. *Laser Light*. illustrated by Radu Vero. New York: McGraw-Hill, 1978.

Stoff, Joshua. *The Voyage of the Ruslan: The First Manned Exploration of Mars*. New York: Atheneum, 1986.

Veglahn, Nancy. *The Mysterious Rays: Marie Curie's World*. illustrated by Victor Juhasz. New York: Coward, 1977.

METRIC TABLE

This table tells you how to change customary units of measure to metric units of measure. The answers you get will not be exact.

LENGTH

Symbol	When You Know	Multiply by	To Find	Symbol
in	inches	2.5	centimeters	cm
ft	feet	30	centimeters	cm
yd	yards	0.9	meters	m
mi	miles	1.6	kilometers	km

AREA

Symbol	When You Know	Multiply by	To Find	Symbol
in^2	square inches	6.5	square centimeters	cm^2
ft^2	square feet	0.09	square meters	m^2
yd^2	square yards	0.8	square meters	m^2
mi^2	square miles	2.6	square kilometers	km^2
	acres	0.4	hectares	ha

MASS (weight)

Symbol	When You Know	Multiply by	To Find	Symbol
oz	ounces	28	grams	g
lb	pounds	0.45	kilograms	kg
	short tons (2000 lb)	0.9	tonnes	t

VOLUME

Symbol	When You Know	Multiply by	To Find	Symbol
tsp	teaspoons	5	milliliters	mL
Tbsp	tablespoons	15	milliliters	mL
fl oz	fluid ounces	30	milliliters	mL
c	cups	0.24	liters	L
pt	pints	0.47	liters	L
qt	quarts	0.95	liters	L
gal	gallons	3.8	liters	L
ft^3	cubic feet	0.03	cubic meters	m^3
yd^3	cubic yards	0.76	cubic meters	m^3

TEMPERATURE (exact)

Symbol	When You Know	Multiply by	To Find	Symbol
°F	Fahrenheit temperature	5/9 (after subtracting 32)	Celsius temperature	°C

METRIC TABLE

This table tells you how to change metric units of measure to customary units of measure. The answers you get will not be exact.

LENGTH

Symbol	When You Know	Multiply by	To Find	Symbol
mm	millimeters	0.04	inches	in
cm	centimeters	0.4	inches	in
m	meters	3.3	feet	ft
m	meters	1.1	yards	yd
km	kilometers	0.6	miles	mi

AREA

Symbol	When You Know	Multiply by	To Find	Symbol
cm^2	square centimeters	0.16	square inches	in^2
m^2	square meters	1.2	square yards	yd^2
km^2	square kilometers	0.4	square miles	mi^2
ha	hectares (10,000 m^2)	2.5	acres	

MASS (weight)

Symbol	When You Know	Multiply by	To Find	Symbol
g	grams	0.035	ounces	oz
kg	kilograms	2.2	pounds	lb
t	tonnes (1000 kg)	1.1	short tons	

VOLUME

Symbol	When You Know	Multiply by	To Find	Symbol
mL	milliliters	0.03	fluid ounces	fl oz
L	liters	2.1	pints	pt
L	liters	1.06	quarts	qt
L	liters	0.26	gallons	gal
m^3	cubic meters	35	cubic feet	ft^3
m^3	cubic meters	1.3	cubic yards	yd^3

TEMPERATURE (exact)

Symbol	When You Know	Multiply by	To Find	Symbol
°C	Celsius temperature	9/5 (then add 32)	Fahrenheit temperature	°F